BLOWN COVERS

NEW YORKER COVERS
YOU WERE NEVER MEANT TO SEE

FRANÇOISE MOULY

ABRAMS, NEW YORK

To my grandmother, Mina, whose spirit inspires me; to my mother, Josée Giron, who always knew to be as smart and brave as she's beautiful; and to my daughter, Nadja, whose intelligence and heart light up the future.

Editor: Eric Himmel
Designer: Françoise Mouly
Design Manager: Kara Strubel
Production Manager: Anet Sirna-Bruder with Ankur Ghosh

Cataloging-in-Publication Data has been applied for and may be obtained from the Library of Congress.
ISBN: 978-1-4197-0209-9

Endpapers: Christoph Niemann
Frontispiece: Art Spiegelman
Case front drawing: Barry Blitt
Case back drawing: Art Spiegelman

Printed and bound in the United States
10 9 8 7 6 5 4 3 2 1

Abrams books are available at special discounts when purchased in quantity for premiums and promotions as well as fundraising or educational use. Special editions can also be created to specification. For details, contact specialsales@abramsbooks.com or the address below.

THE ART OF BOOKS SINCE 1949

115 West 18th Street
New York, NY 10011
www.abramsbooks.com

TABLE of CONTENTS

INTRODUCTION: COVERS UNCOVERED...............4

RACE & ETHNICITY........................18

SEX.................................28

RELIGION...................................40

POLITICS....................................48

CELEBRITIES..............................78

WAR & DISASTERS...........................90

IS NOTHING TABOO?....................................112

BIOGRAPHIES & INDEX....................122

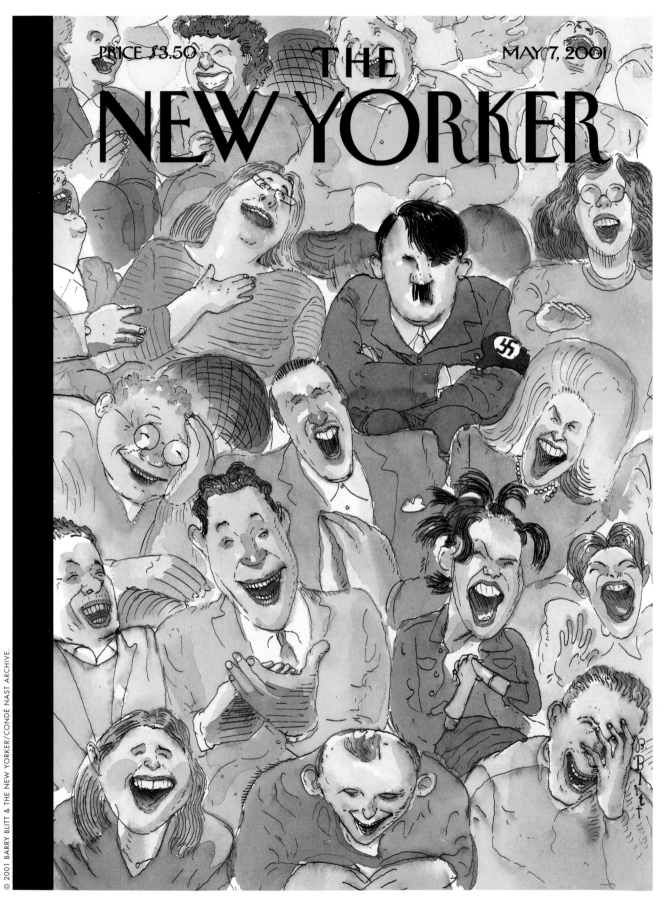

COVERS UNCOVERED

On the twentieth floor of the Condé Nast Building in Times Square, animated billboards shine outside the large windows; yet, as visitors walk toward my office they invariably turn to look the other way. On the corridor wall, arranged floor to ceiling, is every *New Yorker* cover published over the eighteen years I've worked as the magazine's art editor. Inside my office, too, the wall is plastered with sketches, but, if the corridor is a chronicle, the inner wall is a laboratory of ideas. There the arrangement is chaotic, kaleidoscopic: an ever-shifting bulletin board.

On this particular day, in 2001, the visitor is Barry Blitt, one of the rare cartoonists I work with who is actually funny in person. If I had to generalize, I'd say the average cartoonist tends toward the gloomy and retiring; the most common chatter among artists at our parties is about Bristol board, pen nibs, and which anti-depression meds they are on.

Barry, who has come to show me a handful of sketches, is a short bearded man. Standing there in his hat and shorts, he locks eyes with me and smiles, as if to say: "Oh yeah? Just try to mock me!" Barry immediately starts scanning my office wall. It is late April, so the board is packed with springtime sketches, one area devoted to Mother's Day ideas, another to blooming rooftop gardens. I watch his back as he looks. I note which ones make him laugh and, more important, which make him curse with frustration: Nothing inspires artists more than wanting to top someone else's good idea. He pulls out his notebook.

"You asked for something about Mel Brooks's new musical, *The Producers*," he says, showing me a theater audience, all laughing except for one sullen young skinhead.

"I don't get it," I say, leaning over the image.

"Well . . ." He reaches over and peels just the punk off the page, revealing underneath an angry Hitler in the audience. "Originally I had it this way," he says, "but you just can't put Hitler on the cover of *The New Yorker*, can you?"

"But it's perfect that way!" I say. Then I pause and make a quick, silent calculation: *The Producers* has just opened to rave reviews, so Barry's image would work best for the cover going to press this week, out next. But it's already Tuesday and I just sent this week's cover to the printer.

Still, the cover won't actually be printed until Thursday night.

I've got to move fast.

I take a rare chance and ask Barry to stay where he is, sitting on my couch. I run over to David Remnick's corner office. Fortunately, the door is ajar and David is in, sitting

Barry's sketches, with, below, the punk "flap" lifted to reveal the real audience member who is NOT laughing.

A page from L'Assiette au Beurre, *a French weekly satirical magazine from the turn of the last century: A French artist portrays the British love for their king, Edward VII, in the September 28, 1901, issue.*

Cover of RAW 1: The Graphix Magazine of Postponed Suicides, *July 1980, cover by Art Spiegelman, partly printed on my press.*

behind the desk in his spacious, light-filled office, reading a manuscript. Courteous, smart, and handsome—exactly who you'd cast as the head of a refined literary magazine in the movie version—Remnick is what we call in New Yorker-ese (where less is more) the editor. For the covers, at least, there are no editorial meetings, no one else to win over—what he says goes. I knock and he looks up.

"Oh, oh! You've got that grin on your face."

I walk in saying nothing and hand him the unsanitized version of Barry's drawing. He bursts out laughing. I'm reminded of why I think I've got the best job in the world: I get to conspire with some of the funniest cartoonists around just to make my boss laugh. David asks if we can get it done in time for this week's issue, and I run back to my office. Now comes the hard part: After sending Barry on his way to quickly do a rendered finish, I'm going to have to call the artist whose cover I just bumped.

REJECTION IS WITHOUT A DOUBT the hardest part of my job, not only for the artists but even for me. As an editor, I must instill confidence in artists and be a convincing cheerleader: "RAH! RAH! RAH! You can do it! Drop everything else, go face a blank sheet of paper, and send me three great ideas within the hour!" But even as I cajole artists to come up with ideas, I know we won't be able to publish most of them—a weekly only has one cover a week, after all. Some artists just strive to jot thoughts down, regardless of whether they're right for publication. "Don't edit yourself," I tell artists, "Just send it in and let us figure it out." Sometimes, it is through the unfiltered brainstorming sessions that the best ideas emerge. Often, we end up with an overflow of good sketches that we can't use—some simply because the timing couldn't be made to work. I value them all and don't want to lose track of them, so I devote one corner of my office to hilarious but thoroughly unpublishable submissions—unpublishable, that is, until the day, a year or two ago, when Dan Clowes walked in.

A highly respected cartoonist, Dan lives in California but, like many artists, he'll stop by the office whenever he's in New York. After looking at the sketches on the main wall of my office (when he looks, a twitch or a chuckle is high praise), the tall, lean Clowes, a master of understatement, turned to look at the corner of the *refusés*. Chuckling, he said, "You have a book here." And he was right. These crude sketches—a glimpse under the papal robes, Anthony Weiner hanging himself with a noose made of sausage links—are far from the rejected by-product of my work as an editor. They are its lifeblood. These sassy, funny, vital outbursts not only provide the germ from which more refined ideas spring, but they also shed light on the monumental work the artists engage in, week after week, as they ponder our world and its follies in search of ideas. It fascinates me that, collectively, artists so often manage to deliver just the right uncanny image. It's easiest to see that process by rifling through the piles of sketches that came close and didn't work, or through the hilarious ones that just weren't meant for publication. So here it is: the brilliant, the silly, and the profound all mixed together.

MY LOVE AFFAIR WITH FUNNY PICTURES goes back a long way. As a young woman in the early seventies, I studied architecture at the École des Beaux-Arts in Paris. I quickly became frustrated by what I saw as a nearly unbridgeable gap between what an architect can do on paper and the reality of what she will see built in her lifetime. I thought I would sidestep my frustrations by coming to New York for a short stay, but I fell in love and could never go back. First I fell in love with the endless possibilities of the anarchic, chaotic, delirious New York of the seventies, but within a couple of years I had met an underground cartoonist, Art Spiegelman, and then I was hooked on far more than that.

Comics and cartoons were at a low point at that time—they were almost universally regarded as trash culture. But Art is a passionate advocate for his chosen medium. He seduced me by reading me the lavish newspaper comic pages of the early twentieth century, Little Nemo and Krazy Kat. Then he showed me the America he grew up in, giving me Harvey Kurtzman's *MAD* magazine and patiently explaining the jokes. (If anything is love, that is!) After experiencing the limits reality imposes on architects, I was dumbstruck by the impact and freedom that cartoonists have, building not just buildings, but whole worlds on paper that can survive for centuries. It began my lifelong love affair with art for reproduction. I enrolled in a vocational school to learn printing, and then bought a small offset press (which we had to hoist onto the roof and then lower into our fourth-floor walk-up SoHo loft). Within a couple of years, in 1980, we launched our own magazine of avant-garde comics, graphics, and cartoons—*RAW*.

Cover of RAW 3: The Graphix Magazine That Lost Its Faith in Nihilism, *by Gary Panter, July 1981.*

FOR TEN YEARS, I PUBLISHED, DESIGNED, AND COEDITED with Art a magazine whose core mission was to give voice to artists who had something to say. In *RAW*, we also published installments of the long comic work that Art had been laboring over all those years: the story of his parents' ordeal in World War II. The first volume of *Maus* came out in book form in 1986, the second in 1991, both garnering critical acclaim. Still, the magnitude of the recognition took us by surprise. *Maus* received a special Pulitzer Prize in 1992, and, in the fall, Tina Brown, who had just been named editor of *The New Yorker* and was looking to reinvigorate the visuals by inviting new artists, came to the *RAW* office to meet us.

Brown was only the magazine's fourth editor, inheriting mostly the legacy of William Shawn, whose tenure lasted from 1952 to 1987. Shawn's *New Yorker* had been recognized for journalistic excellence, but for an editor with such broad interests, he had a unique approach to covers, which he summed up in the following fashion:

> We have fewer covers today that have humor than we did years ago.
> They tend to be more aesthetic and the subject for the most part is
> New York City or the country around New York City. The suburbs,
> the countryside. Sometimes it's just a still life of flowers or a plant.
> It's not supposed to be spectacular. When it appears on a newsstand,
> it's not supposed to stand out. It's a restful change from all the other
> covers, I'd say.

In 1946, the cover of the groundbreaking "Hiroshima" issue, devoted entirely to John Hersey's eye-opening report, was a charming scene of vacationers in New England.

To be quiet and nearly invisible was not Tina Brown's way. She had decided on three artists she wanted to bring to the magazine: Richard Avedon (who became the first *New Yorker* staff photographer), Edward Sorel, and Art Spiegelman. Art proposed an image that ran as a Valentine's Day cover in 1993 (*see page 18*), showing a black woman and a Hasidic Jew in a loving embrace. That first Spiegelman cover caused a media frenzy. Irate readers threatened to cancel their subscriptions, and heated arguments raged everywhere over its meaning and taste. In a multilayered, irreverent, and ironic cover, Brown had found an image that set the tone she wanted for the magazine. Shortly thereafter, she asked me to join the staff as art editor.

TRYING TO FIND MY BEARING IN THOSE EARLY DAYS, I rummaged through the magazine's archives. I was attracted to the decorative qualities of the covers from the twenties; their posterlike immediacy showed how images can be designed to catch your attention on a crowded newsstand. The influences of the "high" arts evident in Shawn's covers (especially in the work of his most prominent protégé, Saul Steinberg) offered a hint of how images could also stand up to scrutiny on a million coffee tables. But it has always been the covers from the thirties through the fifties that I wanted to show to contemporary artists to say "Top that!" Those covers tell a story—like William Cotton's Irish cop who looks suspiciously at a reveler decked out to celebrate Saint Patrick's Day. Such covers show us what urban sophisticates chuckled at decades ago, their attitudes and prejudices, their mannerisms and jokes. I've pushed the artists week after week, believing that they can create images that, looked at from a later vantage point, might give a similarly nuanced and telling portrait of our society.

Pulitzer Prize–winning writer and reporter David Remnick took over after Tina Brown's departure in 1998, and we all—the new editor, the artists, and myself—adapted to a new sensibility. In early 1999, late at home one evening, I brought up to Art a news event I thought Remnick might find worth addressing—if one could find a way. On February 4, 1999, four white police officers in the Bronx, with little apparent provocation, fired forty-one times on Amadou Diallo, a twenty-three-year-old

In a welcome shift, contemporary artists know to avoid rather than exploit ethnic stereotypes. An artist thinking about a Saint Patrick's Day image might now show an Asian American youngster dressed head to toe in bright green—but the Irish cop is no longer de rigueur.

unarmed West African immigrant, killing him. It was a thorny issue, one I had not solicited sketches about: The circumstances of the shooting were hazy, and I, for one, had found myself unable to explain what seemed like a senseless and brutal killing. There had been some public outrage, especially at Mayor Rudy Giuliani's insistence that the New York Police Department was "just about the most restrained police department in the country," but the story was already dropping from the news. Very quickly, Art sketched an idea on a paper napkin. Now I was faced with a quandary. It was late on a Wednesday night, but if we were going to do a cover about Diallo, it shouldn't wait another week. I hesitated but still called Remnick at home, even though it was past midnight. "Hi, David, so sorry, but I just faxed you a crude sketch. Art has what I think is a good idea." I'm forever grateful to Remnick, who gave the okay without much more than the roughest sketch and a verbal description. Art stayed up all night to do the drawing, and, by the end of the next day, I sent the image to the printer.

THE CONTROVERSY ABOUT THE DIALLO SHOOTING was instantly reignited. The police union called a protest outside of our offices: 250 off-duty police officers showed up. The mayor, Rudy Giuliani, denounced the image to the press: "It's a demonstration of something I have been saying for some time—that there is a virulent prejudice against police officers." A *New York Post* editorial personally took the artist to task: "If you are burglarized, or your family is menaced by thugs, you should be consistent. Call Al Sharpton instead of 911. See where that gets you, Spiegelman, you creep." In the week after the cover ran, daily protests against police brutality formed outside police headquarters in Manhattan; they eventually resulted in the arrest of 1,200 people, including former mayor David Dinkins, actress Susan Sarandon, and the Reverend Jesse Jackson.

Saul Steinberg once told me that what he appreciated about this cover was that it was "a picture of a picture." The policeman is the friendly 1940s neighborhood cop—a cop who's there to protect you, whose gun is merely a reassuring prop. And while the image makes reference to the Diallo shooting, it takes us beyond the racial dimension of the incident. Here none of the policeman's targets are black, or rather, they all are—they are all silhouettes, jolly icons of average New Yorkers. I appreciate how difficult it is to make the late-night decision to publish something that could spark this kind of controversy (and to stand behind it

A cartoon in the New York Post *summed up the furor surrounding Spiegelman's cover. Meanwhile, New York City police commissioner Howard Safir called the* New Yorker *cover "irresponsible, outrageous."*

afterward), so moments like this only further my conviction that I have the best job in the world.

THERE ARE MANY FACTORS AT WORK when determining which images are strong and necessary and which are merely gratuitous provocations. Commenting visually on prejudice does risk rearousing or even validating the prejudice itself. Cartoons build new thoughts using, by necessity, a language of instantly recognizable clichés; they often use stereotypes—a businessman always carries a briefcase—and the stereotypes must be deployed carefully.

It may be difficult to remember now, but just after the 1993 bombing of the World Trade Center the media was wary of labeling the men involved as Arab or Muslim extremists. In part, this was because, until that moment, our points of reference for terrorism on U.S. soil were domestic, such as the Unabomber's exploits. But also at work was an understandable reluctance to attribute negative stereotypes to entire ethnic or religious groups. As the trial of the four World Trade Center bombing suspects got under way, we published a cover by David Mazzucchelli (*opposite*) that visualized New Yorkers' whispered fears. The cover was immediately denounced as prejudiced by anti-discrimination groups. In 1999, Noam Chomsky condemned the image and what he saw as the motives behind it this way:

> A crazed child wearing Arab headdress leaps down to destroy [the World Trade Center] with an ugly leer; the children are black, latino, and white, a deft touch, designed to absolve the authors of any charge of racism, while at the same time highlighting the depravity of the ethnic group that is to be despised by right-thinking people.

But try to imagine the jumping child without an Arab headdress. The image falls apart. Where does the attacking child's anger come from? Why would he be trying to destroy the city? Mazzucchelli's image revealed what in words would have been difficult to formulate at the time: The attack was perpetrated by religious extremists at war with our culture.

THE BEST *NEW YORKER* COVERS don't tell you what to think, but they encourage you to think. In 1994, as I do every spring, I was looking for a June wedding cover. But I also hoped for an image that would capture the stirrings of same-sex marriage—discussed in some circles, but so unimaginable to many that the mere visual representation of such a ceremony could be explosive. Jacques de Loustal's simple gay wedding cover brought up thorny issues: We wanted to have one

July 26, 1993

THE NEW YORKER

Price $1.95

party in black and the other in white to make the portrait read as a wedding, yet we didn't want to label one of these men as "the man" and the other as "the woman." Instead we mixed traditional gender stereotypes, making the man in white taller and placing his hand protectively on his partner's shoulder, while putting a somewhat effeminate pencil-thin mustache on the shorter man in black. Staying away from the cliché of the rainbow, I asked Jacques to use a limited palette of black, white, and shocking pink, which made the image feel iconic. Ten years later, when same-sex marriage began to be legalized, the only image we couldn't have run was this one: By then, the representation of two men in front of a wedding cake had become not a statement, but a staple of the *New York Times* wedding announcement section. But back in 1994, as Yale history professor George Chauncey says, "I know for a fact that it heartened many advocates of gay marriage and marriage equality to see as distinguished a publication as *The New Yorker* put such an image on its cover. I can only imagine that many non-gay readers of *The New Yorker* were startled by [it] but it also made the idea more real, more imaginable to them. . . . It seemed like one of the first and still very rare signs that established heterosexual

liberal opinion might possibly change on this issue." Incisive cartoons, tolerant as they are of ambiguities and internal contradictions, can provide a touch point for change.

SOME COVERS MAKE CLEAR, CONTROVERSIAL POINTS: This is a luxury especially afforded to *The New Yorker* because our covers are signed—they express the point of view of the individual artist, then, and not the magazine as a whole. Often the wit of an artist can cut to the core of complex and touchy issues. When Blitt first showed me his sketch for a cover of Iranian president Mahmoud Ahmadinejad (*overleaf*), he said, "But of course you can't show a world leader on the pot." But Blitt's idea had layers of meaning that made it far from sophomoric. In June 2007, months before this cover ran, Republican senator Larry Craig, who consistently opposed gay-rights legislation, was arrested for soliciting sex from an undercover policeman in an airport men's room. In late September, Ahmadinejad visited the United States. Tensions surrounding Iran's nuclear capabilities were high, but news coverage erupted when, at a forum at Columbia University, the

Iranian president responded to a question about Iran's executions of homosexuals by saying, "In Iran, we don't have homosexuals like in your country. In Iran, we do not have this phenomenon." To comment on either of these news events individually could have amounted to publishing a political cartoon—Ahmadinejad in drag, say, or an elephant at a urinal. Political cartoons have their place; they're very direct, but in their need to label each representation, they often lack the complexity we look for in a cover.

Blitt's image goes beyond "potty humor": The open newspaper gives context and serves as a fig leaf, the tiled floor gives the perspective of a Vermeer painting, and Ahmadinejad's puzzled expression, like a laugh track, provides the viewer with an entry point. This image doesn't target Iran's nuclear ambitions or homophobia. Rather, it asks us to see the Iranian president as a fallible politician, who either does not see or chooses not to see what is right at his feet.

WHEN THE WORLD IS ESPECIALLY GRIM, the professional compulsion to find the right image can be cathartic. Like me, the artists I work with appreciate the opportunity to work in the face of disaster, even if we know that an image alone can't heal a case of the flu, much less a nuclear meltdown in Japan or an earthquake in Haiti. Just bearing witness is a release. But on September 11, 2001, I suddenly found myself without the means, without the distance, to say anything at all. That morning, I saw the first plane ram into the World Trade Center. Art and I ran downtown to get our fourteen-year-old daughter from where she'd just begun high school at the foot of the towers. The three of us watched the second tower fall in excruciating slow motion. Not long after, I was back in my office, trying to find a cover for the magazine. It felt impossible. I resisted the task with every fiber of my being. Images seemed suddenly powerless to help us understand what had happened. The only solution I could find was to run no cover at all—an all-black cover. I called Art to tell him that I was proposing an all-black cover, and he suggested adding in the two towers, black on black. From my first unedited impulse emerged a cover (*overleaf*) that in its simplicity and sobriety managed to express a feeling that had felt unexpressible. Borrowing one of the most abstract, nonrepresentational techniques of modern art, Ad Reinhardt's black on black, the cover conveyed something about the unbearable loss of life, the sudden absence in our skyline, the abrupt tear in the fabric of reality. A colleague later told me he felt the issue we published that week had renewed our readers' trust in the magazine; I know it renewed my own trust in the power of images.

I TEND TO THINK THAT THE THOUSANDS OF WORDS each picture is proverbially worth are better left unspoken. I tell artists that their image isn't ready until it can be shown without a caption. Cartoons freely mix metaphors and part of their strength in breaking through the verbiage is that their impact is hard to

Above: a cover by Lorenzo Mattotti, commemorating the 50th anniversary of the Nagasaki and Hiroshima bombings. Below: RAW *artist Gary Panter sketched from his Brooklyn roof as the towers burned, September 11, 2001.*

PRICE $3.50

THE NEW YORKER

SEPT. 24, 2001

describe. In the relatively recent past, Barry Blitt sent a sketch of the papal skirts being lifted à la Marilyn, the one on the cover of this book; Remnick, who was out of town on a trip, laughed but asked me to gather some other opinions. For once, I found myself in the position of the many art directors who have to lobby for an image while the word people talk themselves out of it. I showed the sketch and everyone laughed, but was soon told that the image didn't work—neither the Pope nor the scandals plaguing the Catholic Church had anything to do with Marilyn Monroe. "Oy vey!" said Blitt, before moving on. The raw strength of any image has a hard time surviving the compromises that a committee review inevitably brings about, and then the moment passes. It makes me even more appreciative of the directness of the decision-making process that Remnick preserves at *The New Yorker*.

AND SO I TACKED THE EXPOSED pontiff back in the far corner. I love them all, those images on my wall, publishable or not, and they're too good to keep to myself. Hence, this book: It's a celebration of the images that throw open the closed bathroom door and let you see for yourself what's inside. It's a celebration of the unique platform that *The New Yorker* offers to visual artists and of the clever readers who respond so passionately, but mainly, it's a celebration of my partners in crime, all the artists who spend hours at their drawing tables coming up with the Pope's underwear, Monica Lewinsky's lollipop, or the gay soldiers' kiss in Kabul. So thank you, David, and thank you, Barry, Ana, Art, Anita, and all the others. May these sketches inspire jealous frissons in all of you (I'll be watching your back!) and may those in turn give rise to many more new published—or unpublished—witty, funny, touching, or outrageous *New Yorker* covers.

"I wasn't trying to make history," said the sixty-three-year-old mother, "I just wanted a baby." Meanwhile, Ian Falconer had found his Mother's Day image for 1997.

FRANÇOISE

I MISS YOU (THE WAY AN ARTIST MISSES AN ART EDITOR). WILL BE IN TOWN TOMORROW AND IF YOU'RE NOT TOO BUSY WILL STOP BY BRIEFLY (WITH AN ADMITTEDLY SMALL PILE OF OLD, DULL, SKETCHES)

YOURS

B. BLITT

RACE & ETHNICITY

ART SPIEGELMAN ON HIS "HASIDIC KISS" COVER:

"I set out to look for a drawing that would somehow shatter Eustace Tilley's sangfroid and his monocle. Considering *The New Yorker*'s tradition of turning to seasonal and holiday themes for its covers, Valentine's Day—a celebration of sentimentality with a vague hint of sex—seemed like a promising peg for an explosive picture.

"I thought about close-ups, faces of unlikely lovers kissing Tilley, and I aimlessly mixed symbols together like a mad chemist to see what might explode. When I doodled Tilley as a Hasidic Jew embracing a black woman I had one of those rare eureka moments. The smoldering resentments between New York's black and Jewish communities had come to a boil in the Crown Heights neighborhood of Brooklyn two years before, erupting into race riots and murder.

"As Valentine's Day approached, the staff was heatedly debating the cover with Tina Brown, the editor. I felt as if I'd been strapped to a roller coaster: It was killed one day and resuscitated the next. On the afternoon the issue was set to go to press, I went to meet a half dozen or so editors, most opposed to my image. Some objected because the magazine could be seen as condescendingly peering down at benighted minorities. I argued that *The New Yorker* could no longer maintain its Olympian pose above the fray of the city's life. Finally, there came an exasperated cry: 'We've got to have *a* cover on press in the next five minutes.' I must have been winning the argument at that moment, and the die was cast."

JEWS EVERYWHERE

"Many voices came forward to express delight with the cover as well; my favorite was from a young reader who wrote that she didn't understand the controversy. She thought that it was sweet of the magazine, on the week of Abraham Lincoln's birthday, to show him kissing a slave."

—ART SPIEGELMAN

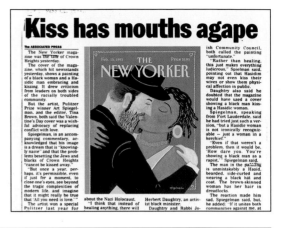

Kiss has mouths agape

THE ERA OF TINA BROWN'S new *New Yorker*, which began with her controversial appointment as editor in July of 1992, saw its first big scandal with Art Spiegelman's "Hasidic Kiss" cover for Valentine's Day 1993. The media coverage that ensued seemed more appropriate to a natural disaster than a provocative image. The magazine had to hire extra office help to contend with the avalanche of "Cancel my subscription!" letters, and security was brought in to deal with more direct threats. Hoping for more such images from the artists I had published in *RAW*, Tina hired me in the wake of the upheaval.

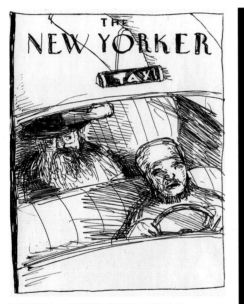

WHEN ASKED IF MAYBE Jews (who do not often show up in his sketches) are just less prone to being mocked, Barry Blitt, who sketched a Hasid in the back of a Muslim cabbie's taxi (*above*), answers without hesitation: "Fuck, no! The right scandal and you'll be seeing Jews everywhere." Art Spiegelman's Hasid has a beard and a belly in common with Santa (*opposite*).

GREG FOLEY is the creative director of *Visionaire*, an influential fashion magazine, which may be why he felt compelled to respond to the scandal that ensued in 2011, when designer John Galliano was videoed publicly spouting anti-Semitic comments (*right*). The model is wearing a Galliano for Dior gown.

PRICE $3.00

THE

NEW YORKER

DEC. 18, 2000

Jan. 30, 1995

The NEW YORKER

Price $2.50

THE RACE CARD

IT ALL STARTED in June 1994 with two murders and a low-speed car chase, filmed from helicopters and broadcast on all channels. O. J. Simpson, nicknamed "Juice," a member of the Hollywood elite and former All-American football player, was apparently fleeing police investigating the murder of his blond ex-wife, Nicole, and her friend Ronald Goldman. There was little time to design covers, and both *Time* and *Newsweek* decided to use the booking photo provided by the police. *Time* called in artist Matt Mahurin for an overnight work session, asking him to make the image moodier. Aiming at a more painterly quality, Mahurin darkened the contrast in areas of the skin. When the magazines appeared side by side on the newsstand, a tempest ensued. *Time*'s managing editor, James R. Gaines, stated that:

> Several of the country's major news organizations and leading black journalists charged that we had darkened Simpson's face in a racist and legally prejudicial attempt to make him look more sinister and guilty, to portray him as "some kind of animal," as the NAACP's Benjamin Chavis put it.

Gaines continued:

> It seems to me you could argue that it's racist to say that blacker is more sinister. To the extent that this caused offense to anyone, I deeply regret it.

Considering the racial tension in the atmosphere and the intensity of the public's reaction to the darkened photograph, the image proposed by Art Spiegelman (*right*), bringing the Ku Klux Klan and minstrels in blackface to the discourse, had little chance of running. It did not make the cover but was published inside with its caption: "Race card trumps gender card when player holds Gold card."

BOB ZOELL'S O. J. cover, published at the start of the trial, did not show the accused man's face, but it worked on more than one level: It was stylistically akin to the quiet *New Yorker* covers of the preceding decades, and the juice glass could be seen as half empty or half full depending on one's point of view (*opposite, and left:* a variant with an empty glass).

DREAMSCAPES

WHEN HAITIAN IMMIGRANT Abner Louima was brutally attacked and sodomized in 1997 by white police officers, many New Yorkers were angered by the mayor's reluctance to investigate the police. Mayor Rudy Giuliani, portrayed in a sketch by Harry Bliss (*opposite*), barely hid his prejudices. In November 1999, the actor and political activist Danny Glover filed a complaint with the Taxi and Limousine Commission, saying that, as a black man, he had a hard time getting a cab in New York; the following Martin Luther King Day found the great man himself stranded on a street corner, in a cover by Barry Blitt (*bottom, left*). For a later MLK Day, Blitt offered a riff on styling white suburban teenagers (*below; middle, left*). In a sketch that Art Spiegelman proposed during George W. Bush's first term, King's dream becomes a nightmare as black leaders like Colin Powell and Condoleezza Rice provide cover for George W. Bush (*below*). In the summer of 2009, a white Boston cop, responding to a 911 call about forced entry, arrested Harvard University professor Henry Louis Gates Jr. at his own residence. President Obama convened a White House "beer summit" among Gates, the policeman, and himself. Blitt sketched what he saw as the conclusion of that "teachable moment" (*left*).

A RABBI, A PRIEST, AND AN IMAM

PLANS TO BUILD A MUSLIM community center in Lower Manhattan went off the rails in the summer of 2010 when a group called Stop Islamization of America dubbed a project that was neither only a mosque nor at Ground Zero, the "Ground Zero mosque." Barry Blitt tried to imagine what would happen if a mosque was built anywhere in New York City, where many of the cabdrivers are Muslim (*left*). Yellow cabs had been on the cover right after September 11 (*opposite*), when Carter Goodrich captured the outpouring of patriotic displays, especially among turban-wearing drivers.

BARRY BLITT ATTEMPTED to portray religious comity, starting out with a rabbi, a priest, and an imam (*above, middle*) on an outing in Central Park. Next, they went boating (*above, bottom*), and finally Blitt had the three going into a bar (*right*). It was a worthwhile attempt, but in the end, it failed to throw much light on the controversy.

SEX

OWEN SMITH ON SEX AND VIOLENCE:

"I had just done this painting of a boxer (*opposite*) and I thought, 'I like the painting, it would be a good cover.' I knew that the editor, David Remnick, has written about boxing, so I was shamelessly thinking, 'Maybe he'll go for it because it's boxing!'

"I get a lot of assignments for sex and violence. I don't know what that says about me. I'm a pretty mild-mannered guy, but I guess I get it all out in my artwork. It's probably the way I paint—there's this robustness to the way the figures are, or they're sexy, or they're sweaty. When it's for *The New Yorker*, people respond: 'Sweaty people! What's that doing on the cover?'

"I did a series of covers for the Fiction Issue. I was coming from a period of pulp fiction paintings, where a cover's meant to grab you, rather than be the kind of polite cover that can be on your coffee table for a long time. People got used to the idea that *The New Yorker* cover's something you live with for a long time, so it's not too offensive. But now we're gonna be in your face a little bit more. It's a different generation and we can be scary music and still be pretty nice.

"We did one for Christmas where the guy has been shot and is lying under the tree. That was more than enough for some readers: 'It's Christmas and you're having murders on the cover? Cancel my subscription!' Those were the covers I got the most comments on. A lurid cover every now and again wakes people up."

UNANSWERED QUESTIONS: *What is the woman doing in the ring, what's her relationship to the boxer, and, an especially salient question considering that a viewer follows the characters' eyes, what are they both looking at?*

SHOW AND TELL

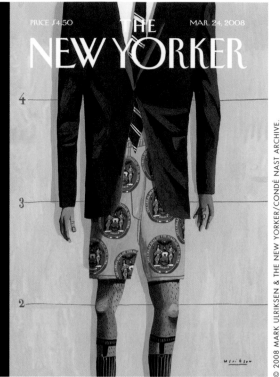

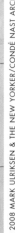

SEX SCANDALS can be a bonanza for magazines, especially when they involve a politician above suspicion. When Eliot Spitzer, the crusading governor of New York, was caught patronizing call girls in 2008, I quickly solicited sketches. I liked what I saw as Peter de Sève's funny, if harsh, proposal for an appropriate punishment (*above*). But when I called to ask him to move the guillotine lower to better make his point, he demurred, explaining he had only meant his image to read as "off with his head." We had many other sketches and chose Mark Ulriksen's (*right*): the disrobing of a straight-arrow politician brought low by his lust.

KNOWN FOR HER CLEVER use of words, Barbara Kruger is one of the few art world superstars who occasionally does magazine covers (*above*). For an Art Issue of *W*, Kruger used "cover lines" as censor bars, allowing the magazine to display a celebrity in full frontal nudity. Cover lines can explain the image or dress up its intent, but they are not available for *The New Yorker*, where images have to stand alone; Bob Zoell's play on words for college graduates (*right*) might have worked inside the magazine with a caption. Still, we are not above running an occasional sexy image: Istvan Banyai's cover (*opposite*) used tight cropping to celebrate a rite of spring.

PRICE $3.50

MAY 6, 2002

THE
NEW YORKER

MONICA'S LOLLIPOP

WITH THE MONICA LEWINSKY AFFAIR, we entered an era in which a politician's sex drive and misconduct could bring the government low. When the news alleging a sexual affair between the president and a White House intern first broke, in January 1998, my husband, Art, and I were in Paris, on our way to the airport. Early on, it was hard to gauge how much trouble this would mean for the Clinton administration and America, but I realized that it meant immediate trouble for me. I called artists from Paris asking them to fax cover sketches to my house in time for my arrival. After a recent submission of Art's had been rejected, he had sworn that he would never attempt another cover, yet on the flight home he seemed unable to resist sketching. I swept up his sketches along with those of the other artists and went directly to my office, which was, as I'd expected, in an uproar. Art's cover, titled "The Low Road" (*opposite*), was published in mid-February. By the end of the summer, Tina had left and we had a new editor, Pulitzer Prize–winning journalist David Remnick. It was all Monica all the time when Anita Kunz proposed the image below for the most innocent of topics, back to school. Meanwhile Art jokingly offered "Clinton's Last Request" (*right*), which ended up running in the online magazine *Salon*, instead.

To Françoise Mouly

Hi! Hope you're having a good summer. I had an idea for the back-to-school issue. It could be drawn in crayon, very child-like; it's Monica Lewinsky sucking a "Presidential" lollipop. — (referring to both her age, and supposed "activities")
Please let me know if you can use it!
All the best, Anita

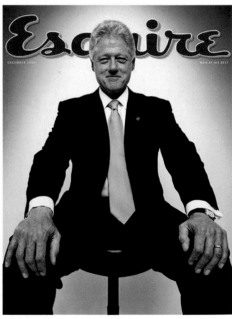

When *Esquire* published a cover portrait of Clinton by Platon (*above*) everyone cried foul, but the photographer asserted that all the image showed was "Clinton loving the fact that he was the *president*."

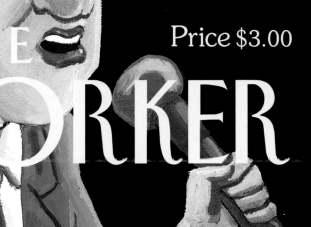

Feb. 16, 1998

THE NEW YORKER

Price $3.00

spiegelman

BIZARRE JUSTICE

THE REPORT THAT PROSECUTOR Kenneth Starr sent Congress about Clinton's relations with Monica Lewinsky was certainly startling: "At one point, the president inserted a cigar into Ms. Lewinsky's vagina, then put the cigar in his mouth and said: 'It tastes good.'" It was difficult to publish, let alone parody, these extremely graphic descriptions, but Barry Blitt did not hesitate to put a cigar . . . in Hillary's mouth (while coiffing her with Monica's beret) (*right*). Art Spiegelman submitted a sketch titled "Bizarre Justice" (*opposite*). The week it would have appeared on the newsstands, Larry Flynt, publisher of the explicit men's magazine *Hustler*, threatened to expose the sexual indiscretions of eleven congressional Republicans.

DOMINIQUE STRAUSS-KAHN, then the head of the International Monetary Fund, was DSK and a presidential contender to the French, but became "Le Perv" (accompanied by a French flag) and "Pepé Le Pew" (a Chuck Jones cartoon skunk in relentless pursuit of "petite femme skunks") for the New York tabloids after he was arrested in 2011 on suspicion of sexually assaulting a hotel maid. Denied bail, he was sent to Rikers Island, which is where Barry Blitt chose to portray him the week of his arrest— with room service at his disposal (*left and right*). Three months later, the prosecutor dropped the charges.

LOVE LESSONS

A "SEXTING" SCANDAL forced Representative Anthony Weiner, one of the Democrats' most effective liberal voices, to resign from Congress in June 2011. Although he was first outed by conservative blogger Andrew Breitbart, Weiner participated in his own demise by fervently denying he'd sent lewd photos of himself to various women (though it was later proven he had). The whole mess was so sordid that the media—and Barry Blitt—didn't hesitate to indulge in "weiner jokes" (*right and below*), though in the end the timing of a double issue prevented us from running a cover on that topic. Blitt had Weiner walking into a landscape populated with Weiner Hot Dogs, Johnson & Johnson, Dick's Sporting Goods, Coq au Vin, a Package Store, Members Only, and a movie marquee featuring *Free Willy* and *Shaft*. Harry Bliss's special-sale image (*opposite*) came unprompted by any news event.

FOR A PLANNED SPECIAL summer issue called "Love Lessons," years before the Anthony Weiner scandal, Art Spiegelman had submitted a beach scene featuring a phallic sand castle (*left*) and later a revision (*below*). Art explains the thinking behind the revision: "When time went by without a response, I got restless and pressed the editor, Tina, who, preoccupied with other things, asked if I had anything about the Kennedy family. Baffled, I resubmitted my sketch with Ted Kennedy's face superimposed on the phallic tower. Tina had somehow never seen my first submission, so my sarcastic Kennedy version totally mystified her."

"I don't think I seriously expected it to get approved, but I submitted it on the principle of 'Nothing ventured, nothing gained.'"
—ART SPIEGELMAN

"If the Internet had existed, I think the 'sailors' kiss' cover would have become a scandal as big as my later White House fist-bump cover."
—BARRY BLITT

AT THE VANGUARD

"Françoise asked me—with little notice—to do a gay marriage cover and the only thing I could think of was gay divorce. I'll do gay divorce for the day it becomes legal." —IAN FALCONER

New Yorker cover of sailors kissing starts another war

By BILL HOFFMANN
A furor has erupted over a New Yorker magazine ...

Today, maybe they do. But that photo belongs to World War II — they ought to keep the save the —

When the Clinton policy of "Don't Ask, Don't Tell" was instituted in 1996, Barry Blitt greeted it with a sailor-on-sailor kiss titled "Don't Ask" (*opposite*). Blitt's take on Alfred Eisenstaedt's photograph of a sailor kissing a nurse in Times Square was denounced at least as much for *The New Yorker* featuring two men kissing on its cover as for its "desecration" of a well-known war image. The legalization of gay marriage in Massachusetts in 2004 prodded Mark Ulriksen's twist on the perennial search for that special wedding dress (*above*). The image proposed by R. Crumb in 2009 (*below*) seemed out of step with its times. And fifteen years after "Don't Ask," in 2011, Blitt's two brides cross the Brooklyn Bridge on their way to City Hall, flower girls in tow, as same-sex marriage becomes legal in New York (*right*).

R. CRUMB IN HIS OWN WORDS:

"I asked my friend Paul, who's gay, if this picture offended him, and he said, 'If I had that, I'd hang it on my wall.'

"The whole idea of this cover is that you can't tell what gender these people are. So what are you supposed to do? Have a gender inspection to see who has what? There are guys who've got their dicks chopped off and girls who've had them added on, so the whole idea of a gender criterion for marriage is ridiculous. At first I thought of drawing two unisex creatures with a minister marrying them—but I drew this thing instead, that was more lurid. I didn't consider it offensive.

"When I was young and full of piss and vinegar, in my twenties, I made drawings with the deliberate intention to offend bourgeois straight people. But then, you can do stuff that you think is just funny and unintentionally offends people—the stuff I did that's considered racist, I didn't do to offend black people or white liberal sensibilities. It was to bring to the surface the underlying cancer that's within all of us whether we know it or not—and for people to see that and maybe laugh at the absurdity of it."

39

RELIGION

IAN FALCONER ON RELIGION:

"I just wanted to do a silly gag, a ridiculous Charles Addams–like situation: 'No room at the inn,' but taking place in one of today's boutique hotels. I should have put Mary on a donkey—it would have been clearer. No special event in the news prompted this image.

"What I liked about the old *New Yorker* covers is that they didn't necessarily have to be timely or topical. No matter what was going on in the world, *The New Yorker* I grew up with, William Shawn's magazine, would probably have a cover of a flowerpot on a windowsill in Cape Cod. At the time, I thought it was better to not bow to the current news cycle; you get dangerously close to being like the other newsweeklies when you do topical covers. But, as an artist, you come up with a gag and you run with it. You know those strange ideas that come to you when you're half asleep in the morning? You're just waking up, still in bed, dozing—you get very vivid oddball dreams.

"My grandmother finally stopped going to church at the end of her life, and she told me, 'I've tried and tried and tried, but I just don't believe it.' Me, I've never tried, though I rather enjoy Roman Catholicism—they put on such a good show.

"It's easier to make a joke about what you know. If I start doing a Yiddish accent, it doesn't play at all—I'd probably do it very badly. I wouldn't be comfortable joking about somebody else's religion. I don't really know much about the born-again Christians, so I can't really make any jokes about that. But the rapture, that would make a funny cover, wouldn't it?"

THE POPE'S UNDERWEAR

IN 1995, THE APRIL 15 tax deadline coincided with Holy Saturday. Art Spiegelman conflated the two for his Easter cover (*right*), sparking protests from a small Christian group. "Mea culpa," said an undaunted Spiegelman to the press. When Spiegelman came into the *New Yorker* offices, David Remnick (then a staffer and a friend) took him to the window to see thousands of people marching down the block, carrying a large crucifix. Spiegelman was disappointed when it turned out to be a Good Friday procession; the dozen protesters were out in the back of the building. Decades prior, in 1966, an extremely controversial *Time* magazine cover featuring a simple three-word question had drawn 3,500 letters, a record for the pre-Internet age (*top*).

THE MOLESTATION and child-abuse scandals hovering over the Catholic Church provided inspiration for Barry Blitt's attempts at lifting the papal skirts (*far left and jacket*). For another image, Blitt chose Father's Day, a perennial theme for *New Yorker* covers—and one that allowed for the use of a greeting card prop to caption the image—to depict a delighted-looking priest surrounded by unsmiling cherubs (*left and opposite*).

THE WAR ON CHRISTMAS

SANTA SEEMS to have been invented for artists who want to depict disillusionment and lost innocence. Norman Rockwell used telltale pieces of the hidden costume in his classic 1956 *Saturday Evening Post* cover (*left*), while in 1946, a department store Santa stars in the great William Cotton's depiction of young boys glimpsing adult reality while their mother's back is turned (*right*). More recently, Walmart proposed the all-inclusive greeting "Happy Holidays" to replace "Merry Christmas" in its marketing, prompting Bill Donohue of the Catholic League and Rush Limbaugh to unleash a media campaign against "the War on Christmas." Bob Zoell, in turn, was inspired to crucify Christmas trees (*opposite*).

IN A SKETCH rejected early on, Art Spiegelman used a jolly Santa to make a point about remembering those in need. When the first version of his image (*right*) was turned down, Spiegelman tried to assuage the editors' qualms by turning Santa around (*above*), leaving room for ambiguity about who had splashed the Christmas tree on the wall. Then, told that the reference to the homeless was what was offensive, Art switched to Santa honoring a bar (*top*). It still was a no-go, so we used it as our Christmas card that year.

CLICHÉS & PREJUDICES

NORMAN ROCKWELL, "the storyteller with a brush," painted 322 covers for *The Saturday Evening Post*, from 1916 to 1963. Rockwell wanted to create iconic American images and thrived on sentimentality. He filled each picture with an abundance of details, each one serving to reiterate the same story

as the picture as a whole. Using the perspective and the cropping of photographs, Rockwell placed the viewer in the space described by his picture: In *Saying Grace*, 1951, the *Post* readers' favorite cover of all time (*top, right*), we are seated at the next table, looking at the woman and young boy praying. It's their obliviousness to everyone around them that tells how absorbed they are in prayer. In his version of *Saying Grace*, Barry Blitt tried equating Islamic with Christian piety (*above*) by changing the protagonists' garb. Rockwell's *Freedom from Want* (*bottom, right*), which was used as propaganda in 1943 to sell War Bonds, beckons us into a scene that, thanks to its snapshot cropping, well illustrates the claustrophobia of a family Thanksgiving. Art Spiegelman repainted it in a sketch in the fall of 2001 (*opposite*), a time of sporadic attacks on American Muslim families. The sketch was accepted, but reports that the United States was, to the confusion of local kids, dropping both cluster bombs *and* care packages in Afghanistan led Spiegelman to choose to commemorate that event instead (*below*).

POLITICS

BARRY BLITT ON POLITICS:

"Even when the topic is deadly serious, you don't want to get too morose or humorless—it's okay for a cover to not be funny but it can't be humorless.

"A lot of the animus against Obama has to do with confounded expectations. No one made those demands on Bill Clinton or George Bush—expecting them to be at their service. I know that, but would it kill Obama to come clean my windows sometime?

"I remember driving up to Canada and listening to lots of talk radio—one right-wing blowhard after another. The hatred for Obama was crazy. He seems kind of namby-pamby and middle-of-the-road to me. I got a note from a fellow illustrator: 'Don't be so quick to put Rush down. You should listen to him sometimes.' I listened to him a lot and my fist-bump cover is not a satire of his position—if anyone knows what satire isn't, it's me.

"That's probably one of the draws of talk radio, that you can say anything. When I got to the U.S. from Canada, I thought Rush Limbaugh was the strangest beast, a true American voice. He was the only one talking like that—this was before Glenn Beck or any of them. But I can't listen to Rush for more than three minutes anymore—he's just infuriating. There's so much anger, so much manufactured rage, and no point. Mostly he's a showman who's pandering."

HOW TO SHOOT FRIENDS

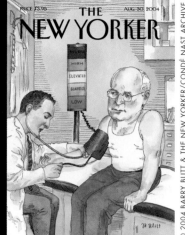

WHEN VICE PRESIDENT Dick Cheney accidentally shot a friend of his in the face during a weekend quail hunt in 2006, he created an easy target for satire. At the White House Correspondents' Dinner in 2009, President Obama quipped that Cheney was "very busy working on his memoirs, tentatively titled *How to Shoot Friends and Interrogate People.*" Barry Blitt took his own potshots at Cheney in this sketch (*right*) and published cover (*far right*).

PRICE $3.99 THE NEW YORKER FEB. 27, 2006

"OOPS"

NO MATTER HOW INSPIRING the topic, only one image can be published every week, and we chose Mark Ulriksen's twist on the poster for the film *Brokeback Mountain*, which had recently been released (*left*). Also in contention were two variants proposed by Barry Blitt (*above and opposite*), both showing the vice president blithely maiming everything and everyone around him. For such a powerful figure as Cheney, the best comedy arose from seeing him misuse an innocuous prop like a TV remote, rather than showing him wounding the Statue of Liberty. For some, that would have felt too close to the truth.

BUSH FATIGUE

WHEN THE OUTCOME of the 2000 election was still in doubt, *The Nation* published a portrait of George Bush as Alfred E. Neuman, the clueless *MAD* magazine mascot (*right*). Eight years later, after two rounds of Bush's presidency, we were still looking for pointed commentary from the artists. Christoph Niemann showed what was left of Bush being squeezed as a sprinkling on the sands of time (*opposite*). Mark Ulriksen painted a lame duck (*bottom, right*). Barry Blitt showed the president playing golf in the White House (*top, right*).

TO THE SURPRISE of many liberals, in late 2008 Karl Rove described George Bush as an avid reader. Bush's love of reading had earlier prevented us from pursuing Barry Blitt's sketch for an end-of-year Fiction Issue (*left*)—it's best when funny ideas are not based on gratuitous prejudice but rather encompass a kernel of truth.

THE 2008 ELECTION

"OLD MEDIA" was Barry Blitt's title for an image of a suspender-wearing Larry King and Republican candidate John McCain, both nodding off (*opposite*). (King retired two years later, "hanging up his suspenders.") Blitt tried a variant in which a younger viewer—and his dog—have also been put to sleep (*left*). The images brought up concerns about ageism, as did Blitt's other sketch (*above*), which showed McCain following the debate between Clinton and Obama from the comfort of his retirement home–issue easy chair.

BY THE SPRING OF 2008, the battle for the Democratic nomination had narrowed down to a contest between Hillary Clinton, the party front-runner, and Barack Hussein Obama, a young and relatively inexperienced African American politician from Chicago. As Obama continued his string of electoral and fundraising successes, Clinton shifted her attacks from Obama's inexperience to his lack of "electability." Clinton's ostensible argument was that Obama couldn't beat a Republican because of his naïveté, but the media was also rife with mentions of the "Bradley effect" (a reference to the discrepancy between voters' intentions and their actual votes in the case of nonwhite vs. white candidates). I talked to Mark Ulriksen about an image of Hillary painting blackface on Obama while McCain contentedly looks on (*right*), but one glance at the sketch showed it oversimplifed nuanced and complex issues without going to the heart of the matter. I kept encouraging artists to jot down and submit more ideas.

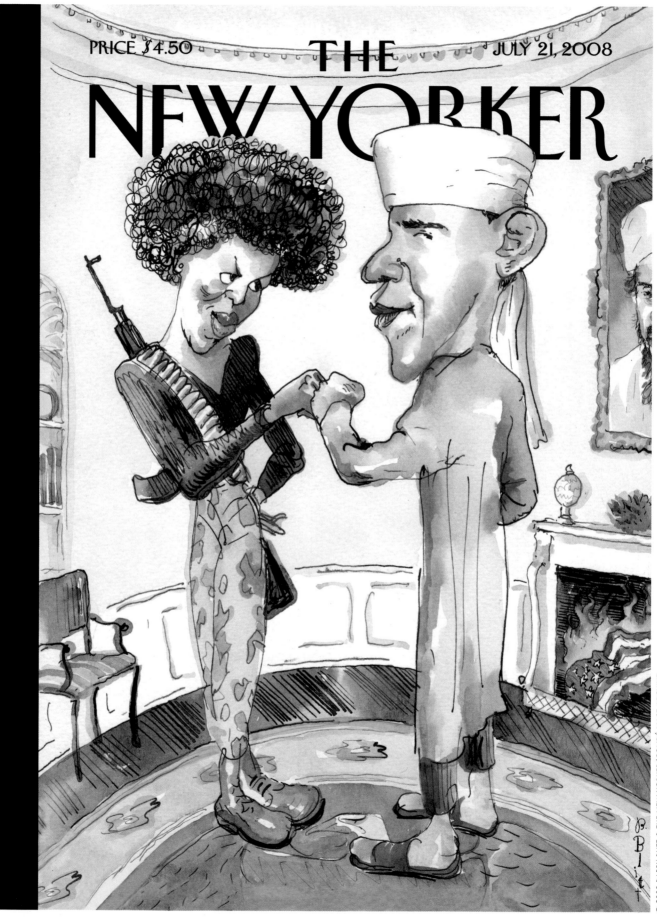

BARRY BLITT · THE POLITICS OF FEAR

© 2008 BARRY BLITT & THE NEW YORKER/CONDÉ NAST ARCHIVE.

RUSH'S WORST NIGHTMARE

BARRY BLITT, WHO OFTEN has pitch-perfect ideas, nailed it when the election pundits started debating which candidate was best suited to answer the White House's red phone in the middle of the night (*right*). I kept hoping for images that would satirize the bigotry, illustrate intangibles such as the reaction to Michelle's "proud of my country" remarks, or the fact that Obama was referred to as "articulate" or as "Barack *Hussein* Obama." Blitt said something about Barack and Michelle exchanging what was then deemed a "terrorist fist jab" in the White House; it sounded funny so I asked for a sketch (*below*). It made the July 21 cover with the title "The Politics of Fear" (*opposite*). Many readers objected, explaining that they understood the joke but were afraid that lesser souls might not. On *Fox & Friends*, Gretchen Carlson was asked why she had not found Blitt's earlier red-phone cover just as offensive as the fist bump. "Yes," said Carlson, "but everyone knows *that's* not happening!" So we gathered that, for her at least, a first lady sporting a machine gun or a president burning an American flag were simply not as ridiculous a thought as Hillary and Barack in bed.

*In the first sketch (*above*), Michelle is also a Muslim, and Ann Coulter, Bill O'Reilly, and Rush Limbaugh are looking aghast through the window at their "worst nightmare." But it didn't seem correct to attribute the prejudices and hidden fears to only those three pundits, so I asked Barry to refine the image to its essence.*

A CONVERSATION

FRANÇOISE MOULY: *What do you remember of the reaction when your "fist-bump" cover was published?*

BARRY BLITT: I remember sitting here playing music with a friend and the phone started ringing a lot. First it was you calling, "They're talking about it on CNN." Then *The Huffington Post* called asking for a quote—and then there were hundreds of e-mails coming in.

FM: *What did you say to your friend?*

BB: Well, I was freaking out, but he was like, "It's a cartoon, so don't worry about it." *The Huffington Post* asked if I regretted it, on Sunday night at 10 P.M. The issue hadn't even come out yet. And I said, "How can I regret it before it's hit the newsstand?" I tried to explain what it was that I was making fun of—the *perception* of him, not *him*. I wish I hadn't said anything and just let it sit there. If I really believed in the image, I shouldn't have had to defend it. If you have the strength of your convictions . . .

FM: *David Remnick used the word* satire *when he went out to defend the cover; that's a tough argument to make because satire has an object—and if the object of satire here is Rush Limbaugh, it's not shown.*

BB: I don't think it has to be shown. I'm sure I could think of a satirical situation where the object isn't shown—if you give me a couple of months. The image probably is clumsy, but it does make me laugh.

FM: *A suggestion came in one of the ten thousand e-mails and letters of protest, someone suggesting we should have put the Fox News logo in the corner. My problem with that is similar to the one I had with putting three right-wing talk show hosts looking in through the window: It restricts the target of the satire to a narrowly defined culprit. One proof to me that your image is not clumsy is that it was effective. The talk of Obama being a secret Muslim abated, and I know of no instances of the image being used by the right wing as a rallying cry.*

BB: *The New Yorker* sure sold a ton of prints. I called Remnick and I said, "David, I worry I'm going to be the darling of right-wingers and skinheads!" And he wrote me back and he said, "Barry, it's a beautiful day, why don't you go out and enjoy it."

FM: *You think the only person who would want to frame this image is someone who believes that it denounces Obama? It was cited in* The New York Times *as the most significant image of the 2008 election.*

BB: I play piano with a guy—his father is a fat old Italian guy, very right-wing. The father said to me, "Hey, I got that picture up on the wall in my office! People look at me, but I say, 'Hey, it's *The New Yorker*!'"

FM: *In 2006, Obama did what all American politicians visiting foreign countries do: He was photographed in local garb, wearing a turban and native Somali clothing during his first visit to Kenya. All politicians do such things but it doesn't make them anti-American; still the* National Enquirer *and* Drudge *published the photo as if it was damning evidence. I think your drawing is clear—but obviously . . .*

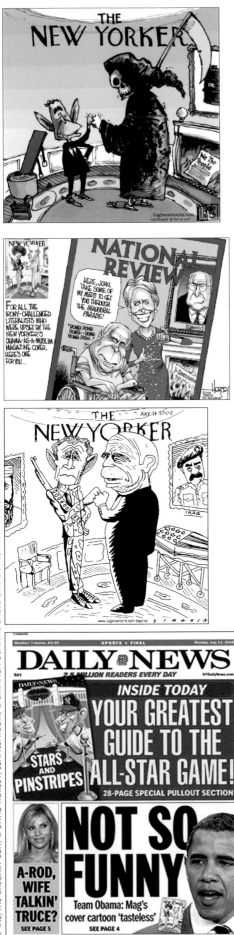

BB: This right-wing guy hates Obama and look—here's Obama depicted in unflattering light, no matter what irony there might be.

FM: *What impact do you think your cover had on the course of the 2008 election?*

BB: None. I don't think it had any impact at all. Maybe it got people talking about this sort of taboo a little bit. But my default position is to think that this did not really make a difference. It's a cartoon and very few minds get changed. Maybe they get changed by seeing a person's character over the long haul. But this is more ephemeral than a snapshot; it's a cartoon. Ultimately, it's a wise-ass reaction to something. Despite the fact that it stuck around for a few days, it came and went. I don't think it unearthed any deep truths.

FM: *You don't think there's something about showing what Rush Limbaugh was saying that scared people out of saying it or thinking it?*

BB: Maybe. But then again, recently there were polls saying that most Republicans still think the president is a Muslim. So what good could the image have done? It's dangerous to start thinking that your work changes things.

FM: *I agree with you on that front. It's as important to do it as it is to not think too much about it. If you're thinking: "I have to find the most important image of the 2008 election," you're highly unlikely to come up with anything that's either funny or relevant. It is one of those paradoxical things where if you find it, you don't turn away from it, but still you shouldn't go taking yourself too seriously.*

BB: When I draw in my sketchbook, I try and draw as badly and quickly as I can and not dwell on it. I don't want to feel like there's too much weight on each page. I just want to spit things out and not worry about it.

FM: *What would happen if you took yourself too seriously?*

BB: I have no idea. I don't think there's a danger of that. I do have my moments, where I walk around in my pajamas saying things. "They didn't take me seriously! Now they'll be sorry! They laughed at me at the Academy!"

FM: *What about all those cartoons parodying yours? Isn't that kind of flattering?*

BB: I have to admit that I don't even look at them. I think you have to be selective—I don't look at everything I see. If you tell me to turn right at the church at the top of the hill, I'll get lost because I just don't notice churches, they've never been of use to me. "What church? There's a church at the top of the hill?" The Jon Stewart/Stephen Colbert one was flattering. But the rest? Anything that's in the news like this is going to get that treatment. Rush Limbaugh had the cover up on his site and he was standing there with paints pretending he was painting it.

FM: *So in a way, it's as if Rush is completing the thought here—he's adding the Fox logo.*

BB: If Rush is mentioned in something, he'll post it even if it's not something he should be proud of. My mother was appalled when the image came out. She called me that Monday and said, "What did you do? You make me sick!" I just hung up on her, it was awful. She's a big Obama fan, she just started yelling. That's how I was brought up, a lot of yelling.

FM: *What about your son, Sam, what was his reaction?*

BB: I came in from the studio—he was monitoring the situation on TV—he was very aware—and he seemed to be kind of protective. He was proud and protective. I didn't know what the fuck was going on, we were sitting down, having dinner, and suddenly we saw our neighbor, who I barely know, walking towards the kitchen window. He was saying, "This is the best thing that could ever happen to you—everyone's talking about it on the train." He thought it was cool. So if I'd killed a little girl—he'd be on the news, man. It wasn't as good as a little dead girl. But it was close.

THE WEEK AFTER the fist bump, one valid response would have been to follow up with another provocative image. John Mavroudis sent a suggestion for self-censorship (*below, right*). Art Spiegelman, who had provided a spirited defense of Barry Blitt's image on the radio, proposed his own version of a follow-up cover, this time targeting Bush and McCain (*below, left*). Since many critics had said that "The Politics of Fear" would have been less offensive if it had run with a caption or a title on the cover to explain itself, Spiegelman ripped off what would have been the unpublishable part of his image and engineered a trompe l'oeil to reveal its title, "'Straight' Talk Express"—also, incidentally, the name of McCain's campaign bus.

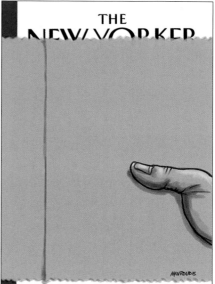

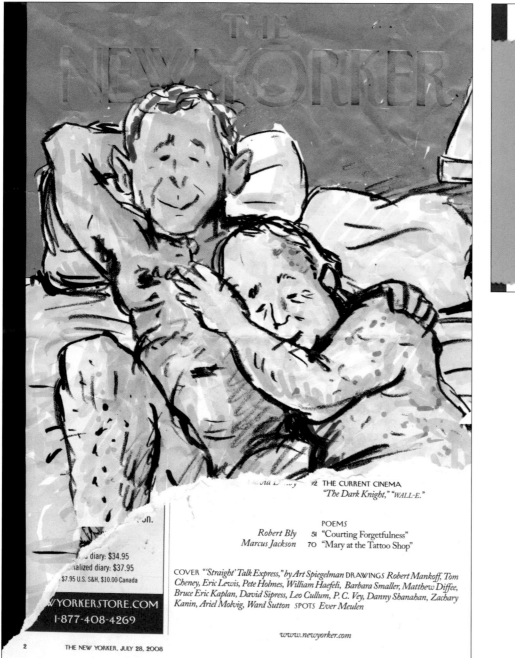

WHEN "POLITICS OF FEAR" was first published, Jon Stewart immediately demonstrated the point the image was making. He broadcast a montage of all the TV clips that implied that Obama might be a Muslim: They came not only from Fox, but also from ABC, CBS, NBC, CNN, virtually every reputable news source. Jake Chessum, the photographer who staged this shot of Colbert and Stewart for a December *Entertainment Weekly* cover (*opposite*), was kind enough to send a print of the image, which now sits, proudly framed, in my office.

STEWART & COLBERT

POLITICS: THE NEW REALITY TV!

Entertainment WEEKLY

#1014 • OCT. 3, 2008

This Crazy Election

MOOSE HUNTS, FIST BUMPS, AND BAILOUTS!

Our Favorite Pundits On
The Most Entertaining
Race Ever

Stephen Colbert
and Jon Stewart
photographed
exclusively for EW
on Sept. 18, 2008,
in New York City

THE BRIDGE TO NOWHERE

"There's just something about Sarah Palin that upsets me. Sometimes you can't argue with a stupid person. It's like a toy super villain absorbing your firepower—you point out their mistakes and it makes them stronger."
–BARRY BLITT

When John McCain introduced his running mate, Alaska governor Sarah Palin, at the Republican Convention, she crowed: "I told Congress, 'Thanks but no thanks,' on that bridge to nowhere." It quickly came to light that Palin had actually once been a leading proponent of the $223 million bridge to an island with . . . fifty inhabitants. Art Spiegelman submitted his own vision of the bridge (*below, right*). Palin quickly grabbed all the headlines, and many artists grabbed their pens. John Cuneo sent in "Palin's cheat sheet" (*opposite*) while Barry Blitt drew McCain as Palin's puppet (*below, top left*). Peter de Sève sent in what he saw as McCain's version of Obama's slogan (*right*). Meanwhile, a Republican political consultant denounced the cover of *Newsweek*, a tight close-up of the former beauty queen (*below, bottom left*). "It's a clear slap in the face at Sarah Palin," she said on Fox News, "Why? Because it's unretouched."

THE VIEW FROM MY WINDOW

TINA FEY'S PARODY of Sarah Palin on *Saturday Night Live* seemed more real and believable than the candidate herself. Although Palin did tell ABC's Charles Gibson, "They're our next-door neighbors and you can actually see Russia from land here in Alaska," it was in a comedy sketch featuring Tina Fey as Palin that the line was immortalized as, "I can see Russia from my house!" The phrase inspired Barry Blitt (*opposite*), who added a reference to "View of the World from Ninth Avenue," a classic *New Yorker* cover by Saul Steinberg. As Palin advocated shooting wolves from a helicopter, Eric Palma sketched a gun-wielding Cheney handing her the vice presidential baton (*left*), and Blitt imagined the crowd that would show up at her events (*below, left*). Blitt also portrayed her prepping for interviews with the books that had served George Bush so well—*My Pet Goat* is the book Bush had been reading to kindergartners when an advisor told him about the attack on the World Trade Center on September 11, 2001 (*below*).

"I think it might go back to high school—that overconfidence of the jock and the pretty girl—there's just no self-awareness or irony."
—BARRY BLITT

PRICE $4.50

THE
NEW YORKER

OCT. 6, 2008

PLUS ÇA CHANGE...

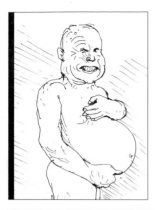

WITHIN DAYS OF MCCAIN choosing Palin as his running mate, the news broke out that Palin's seventeen-year-old daughter, Bristol, was pregnant and had chosen to keep the child and raise it with the support of her family.

"So suddenly pregnancy is an issue. It was a kind of double step: It seemed that McCain immediately started to regret his choice of Palin, but now he was pregnant with the situation. And also, McCain had denounced Obama as just a celebrity, but he couldn't have picked a more empty, celebrity-type VP."
–BARRY BLITT

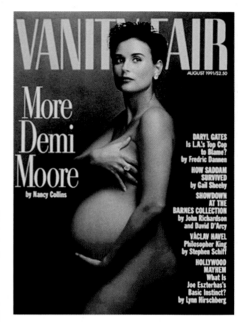

Top left and opposite: Barry Blitt was parodying the 1991 cover of *Vanity Fair* that then-editor Tina Brown had commissioned from Annie Leibovitz (*above*). The groundbreaking image had heralded a new attitude toward pregnant bodies.

IN HER acceptance speech for the vice presidency, Palin said, "What's the difference between a hockey mom and a pit bull? Lipstick." A week later, in a campaign speech, Obama said, "John McCain says he's about change too. . . . That's not change, that's just calling the same thing something different. You know, you can put lipstick on a pig, but it's still a pig." The Internet was instantly awash with red lips painted on photos of Obama, Hillary, McCain, and pigs. Meanwhile, artists sent sketches: John Cuneo (*left*) used the idea of lipstick to represent the trace of kisses left by McCain as he hugged Bush in a well-known photo (*right*).

THE LONG ROAD

THE COUNTDOWN to the November 2008 election gave way to a moment of pure joy for the country's liberals, and many artists sent me one celebratory image after the other. *Right* and *opposite*: Barry Blitt's fist bumps. Brian Stauffer's long red tunnel with a hint of blue light at the end was the image on the stands the week the voting took place (*below, left*). Bob Staake's memorial cover right after (*below, right*) became an all-time bestselling *New Yorker* cover print.

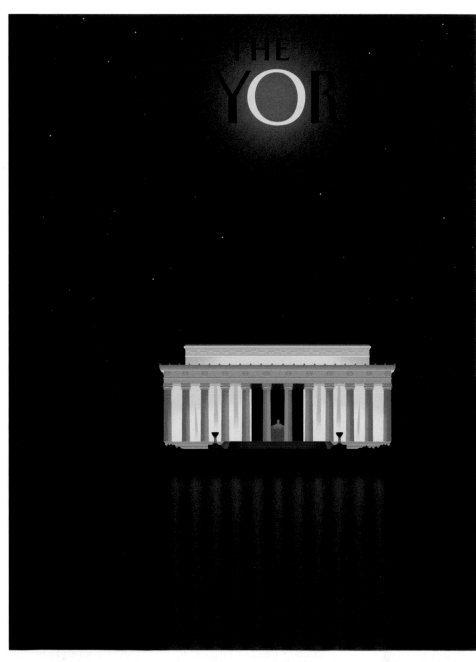

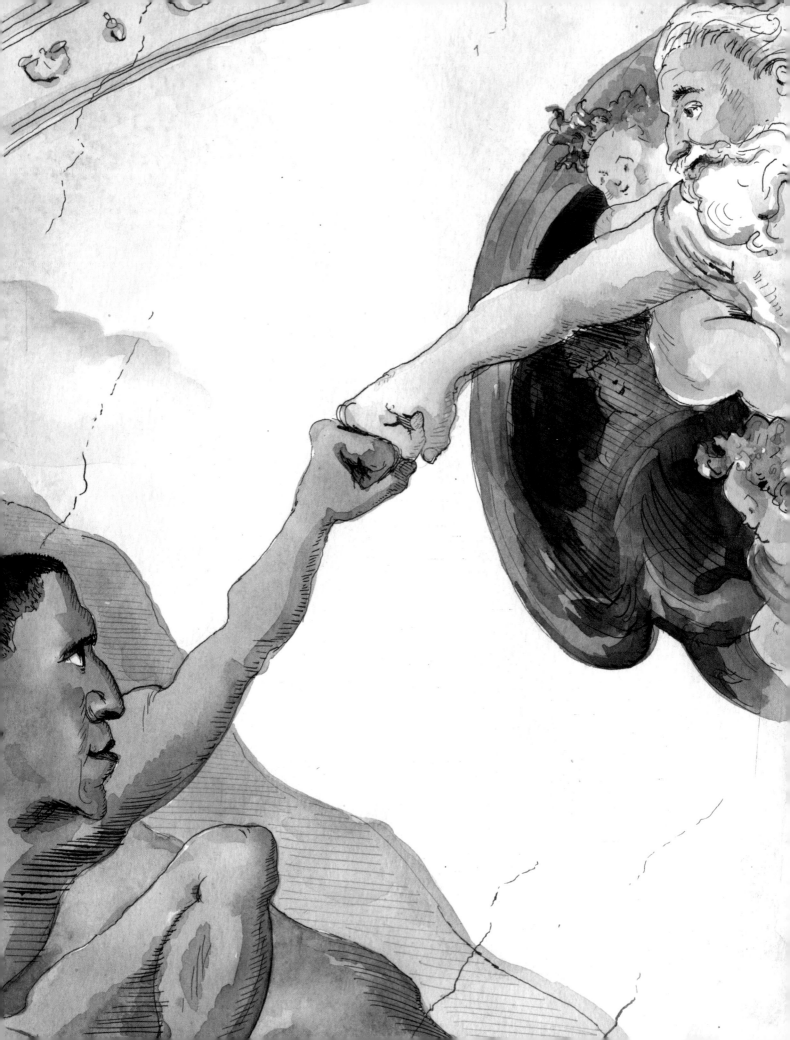

ALL THE PRESIDENTS

IT TAKES TIME for the public at large to form its own impression of a new president and for cartoonists to find ways to represent him. At the start of Obama's term, sketches came in which showed Obama as Roosevelt, Lincoln, or Kennedy. Robert Risko contributed Obama as Roosevelt and on a dollar bill (*opposite* and *below, left*). In just one sketch, Barry Blitt added Obama as Bush, Reagan, Taft, and Nixon (*right*). Drew Friedman portrayed him as Washington for a cover published for the inauguration in 2009 (*below, middle left*), and Ana Juan showed another president, Lincoln, wearing an Obama pin (*below, middle right*).

"When I draw someone, I really try to get their likeness down—I have to find the most refined simplistic immediate recognizable image for that person. One of my tests for that is to silhouette the face and fill it all in black—can you still tell who the person is? The shape should read as a bar code in the brain."

–ROBERT RISKO

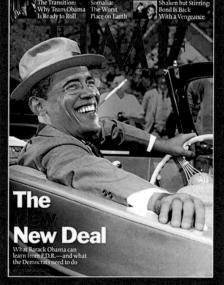

SOME IDEAS are simply in the air: Obama as Roosevelt by Robert Risko (*opposite*), and on the cover of *Time* (*above*).

CLEANUP TIME

IN THE WAKE of the election, artists needed to find acceptable ways to represent this president, who functioned as the repository of so many people's hopes and expectations. Bob Staake painted him as a paper doll that could be dressed either as an angel—complete with halo and harp, or as the devil—with horns and trident (*right*). Anita Kunz sketched Obama inheriting eight years of Republican mess (*below*)—but it simply was not justifiable to show our first black president as a janitor. Barry Blitt's sketch of Bush handing Obama the keys to a totally wrecked car (*opposite*) came close to being approved—till we realized that the setting could be seen as showing the new president in the position of a parking attendant. Still, Blitt observed, "You can't concentrate on Obama's blackness—I mean he's a less black president than Bill Clinton was."

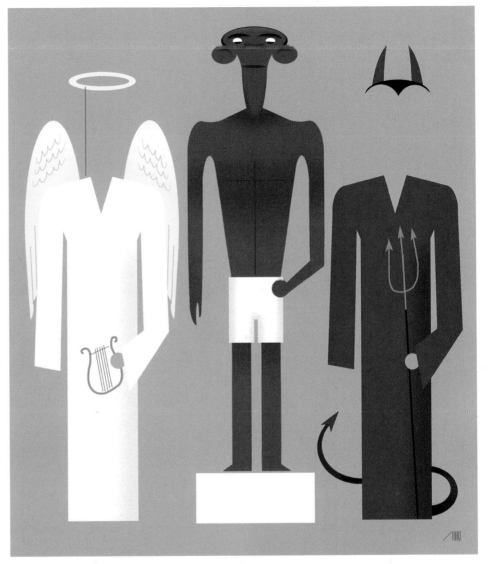

BOB STAAKE ALSO TRIED mocking Obama for his smoking habit (which the president reportedly had trouble giving up) (*left*), but then we saw a hyperrealistic cartoon of the very same idea on the cover of *MAD* magazine (*above*).

ENTER THE TEA PARTY

"Obama with a Hitler mustache was all over the news. Sometimes something makes you laugh and you don't even really want to figure out why. I did draw this before I figured it out. I guess the image is about icon status—it's saying Obama's as much the Mona Lisa as he's Hitler, and the Mona Lisa is the ultimate celebrity."

–BARRY BLITT

BARRY BLITT imagined Hitler mustaches on *all* presidents (*right* and *below*). *Time*'s Man of the Year format (*left*), an extremely powerful style of magazine cover that lasted for decades, familiarized the public with the likenesses of generations of world leaders.

THE TEA PARTY introduced new visual vocabulary. What can an artist do with a teacup? Bob Staake used a simplified palette to show a teakettle's post-nasal drip into a cup (*opposite*). Barry Blitt had the new president stubbing out his cigarette in one (*above*).

HEALTH CARE

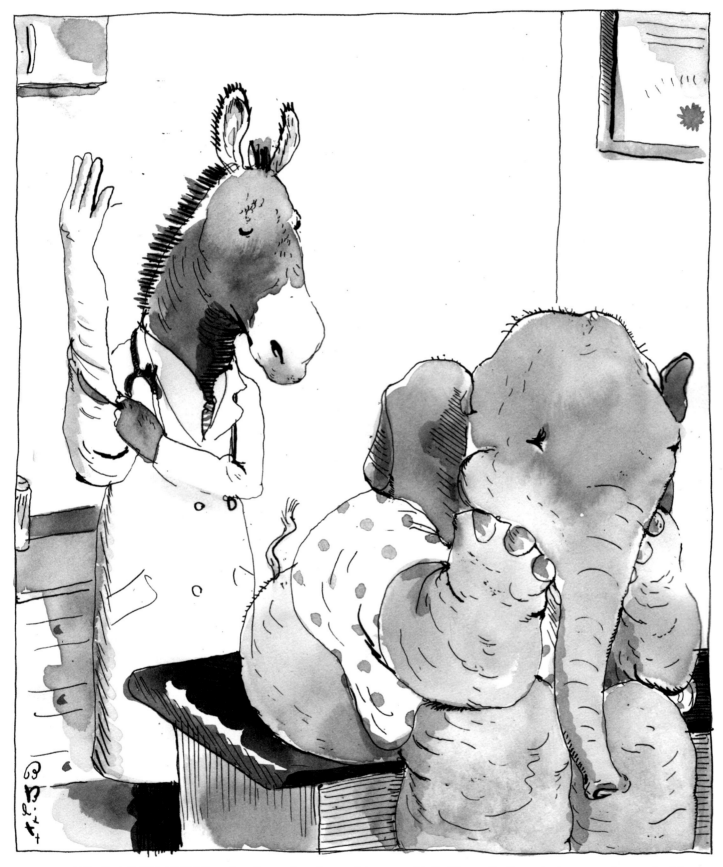

AFTER A YEAR OF FIGHTING and endless scaling down of the original bill, Obama finally pushed a comprehensive health care bill past the reluctant Republicans. Seen here are Lou Romano's proposed image for the occasion (*left*), and Barry Blitt's, which is a tad naughtier (*above*).

CELEBRITIES

ROBERT RISKO ON CARICATURING CELEBRITIES:

"I've always been able to draw people since the time I was five years old. I tried teaching a class for a while and I found it difficult—you just can't teach people. I know other caricaturists and they, like myself, simply felt compelled to put down what they saw in other people's faces. I don't know if it's a gift or a bodily function—it's just something you have to do. I would rather draw people with graphic features—give me a blonde and I panic. I love strong shapes and sweeping contours.

"For *The New Yorker*, if they ever put a famous person on the cover, it has to be within the context of an idea, but to me, a strong likeness is already a concept. To me, some people are always a profile and others have a front-on face, like Palin. Certain celebrities like to be photographed from one side. Only a certain angle of Obama will show his big ears.

"Michael Jackson had just died and I wanted to create an emblematic logo of what he had turned himself into. People become beautiful when they get so scary looking. It's a phenomenon. All icons do that. Even Marilyn Monroe when she got older, her hair went from dirty blond to blond to white, and then she became this vision of white with two black eyeliner lines.

"When people turn into icons—especially sinister ones—it's always a red, black, and white theme. White face, black hair, and red. Michael wore a lot of red—he became Liza, Liz Taylor, the Nazi Party. And it had to be a skull face, a white skull—to me, he was an animated cadaver. There was also the Shroud of Turin—I wanted that. If there was any concept—but it's important that it not be spelled out—it would be that it's a death mask, MJ's death mask."

Since not *having celebrity covers has long been one of the hallmarks of* The New Yorker, *we think hard before breaking that unspoken rule. Ultimately we decided that not having a Michael Jackson cover the week after he died was still our best option.*

THE PEOPLE VS. MICHAEL JACKSON

THE GLOVED ONE on a *New Yorker* cover had been tried before. In the late fall of 2003, the rumors of Michael Jackson's pedophilia exploded again: He was charged with having committed "lewd or lascivious acts" with a child younger than fourteen. In a proposed Christmas image, Barry Blitt quickly pounced on the theme of lost innocence by picturing a child looking quizzically at Michael Jackson as Santa (*right*), who, in turn, seems just as puzzled about what is to happen next.

CHRISTMAS IS PROBABLY NOT the best time for an image about child molestation, so Barry Blitt proposed another image for New Year's Eve (*opposite*), this time alluding to a widely publicized incident from fall 2002. Jackson, who had gone to Berlin to receive an award for his philanthropic work with children, had stepped out onto his hotel balcony and dangled his infant son (whom he affectionately nicknamed "Blanket") above the crowd of assembled fans. Ironically, the star may have been intending to show his fans that he was a good father, or, at the very least, that he was a father. Jackson covered the face of the writhing baby, possibly out of a concern for privacy, giving the impression that if he didn't drop the child, he'd suffocate him. Blitt's image did not show its main subject, but it did take advantage of the easily identifiable Jackson palette: red shirt, white skin, pitch-black hair. And, though Blitt is counting on readers to know the reference, he departs from the facts of the case: Where Jackson had the baby under his arm, Blitt's infant is barely held in dad's hands. And whereas the covered baby face was memorable, Blitt makes a full reveal the center of his composition. The onlookers at the bottom look and point up, and so do we. As the new year starts, we are right there, in the center of the image, mirroring the baby's horrified expression.

LADY-KILLER

THE SUPERMARKET TABLOID *National Enquirer* started it all when it published a small article about an alleged extramarital affair between professional golfer Tiger Woods and a nightclub manager. Five months later, the story was everywhere, as a seemingly endless stream of mistresses was uncovered. The *Enquirer* ran a headline claiming that, over the course of his six-year marriage, Woods had slept with more than 121 different women. "Tiger Woods's whole thing was that he was so wholesome, a clean young man who sponsored many products. You just didn't think of him doing something like this. And the whole scandal just kept getting tawdrier and tawdrier, as more and more women stepped forward," Barry Blitt remembers. "My image (*above and opposite*) is, on the surface, so clean because you really have to have some remove from the tabloidness of a story like this, otherwise it wouldn't seem *New Yorker*-y. To see him in bed with a whole bunch of women, that wouldn't work."

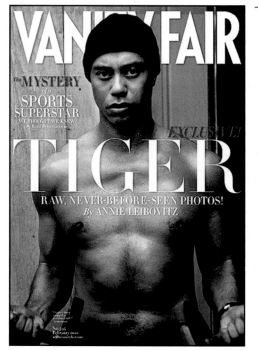

VANITY FAIR'S COVER featuring Woods (*above*), taken pre-scandal by Annie Leibovitz, caused a stir: Was this, as Leibovitz said she intended, a portrait of an "intensely competitive athlete" or, as various bloggers claimed, the portrayal of a hypersexual black man—the racist trope of the black brute?

JOHN CUNEO'S SKETCH of Woods caught in a sand trap (*right*), though at first glance similar to Barry Blitt's, is far less wicked—the reader doesn't have to fill in the blanks.

CELEBRITY COVERS

SOMETIMES celebrity covers are unavoidable—Prince William and Kate Middleton's wedding was hard to ignore. David Remnick liked one of the first sketches that Barry Blitt turned in (*right*), but still asked that no one be seen "doing it" on the cover, royals or not (*far right*). When Arnold Schwarzenegger was elected governor of California in 2003, he was the quintessential American celebrity—a rich movie star married to a Kennedy. He was also the target of allegations of sexual misconduct in what was dubbed "Gropegate," and John Mavroudis put one and one together in a sketch (*right*).

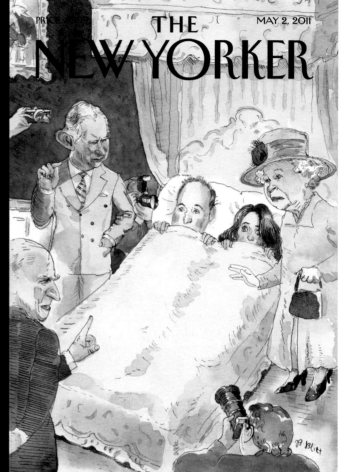

WE LOOK AT images of celebrities with their media personas already in mind. In the hugely popular TV show *Seinfeld,* Kramer (played by Michael Richards) always burst into Jerry's apartment looking surprised, even though there was never any cause for it. In late 2006, Richards unleashed a string of racial slurs against a black heckler during a stand-up routine. In the sketch that Barry Blitt proposed for the next Martin Luther King Day (*opposite*), he used the recognizably funny situation of Kramer walking into a room, but made sure to give Kramer-Richards something to be truly surprised about. Donald Trump's aborted run at the presidency in 2011 lasted just long enough for Blitt to mock Trump's questioning of the legitimacy of President Obama's citizenship (*above*); Blitt also showed nesting birds putting the magnate's signature hairstyle to good use (*left*).

GOOD TASTE PREVAILED

FRUMPY, MIDDLE-AGED Susan Boyle became a worldwide sensation when 75 million people discovered her performance on the show *Britain's Got Talent* on YouTube in 2009. After an awkward encounter with the smirking judges, she ravished them all with her supremely confident singing of "I Dreamed a Dream" from *Les Misérables*, a perfect choice for the launch of a fairy tale. "I know what they were thinking, but why should it matter as long as I can sing? It's not a beauty contest!" she quipped. Barry Blitt's proposed image (*left*) was indeed about "what people think," confronting us with our unexamined assumptions about feminine beauty. He made sure that his proposed model came with the appearance of diversity that is mandatory nowadays.

A CLASSIC *NEW YORKER* CARTOON by Charles Addams, in which a skier is puzzled by parallel ski tracks parting to go around a tree trunk, was Harry Bliss's inspiration when working on a winter sports image (*opposite*). When skiing accidents involving celebrities and trees happened, Harry sketched a few variants on the theme (*above and right*). The accidents had been deadly, so good taste prevailed and we stayed away from any and all.

GUESS WHO'S WATCHING

WHILE EVERY DAY BROUGHT stunning new developments during the Arab Spring in 2011, Barry Blitt submitted a sketch of a Middle Eastern family looking quizzically at American television's coverage of Charlie Sheen's shenanigans (*right*). Glenn Beck, who used the guise of political commentator to build a cult around himself, is a more likely cover subject for us than, say, Lindsay Lohan or Paris Hilton. Illustration student Korwin Briggs proposed using Glenn Beck's blackboard demonstration style to diagram out all that is wrong with *The New Yorker* (*far right*).

IN A PARODY OF a once well-known Coppertone ad (*above*), Barry Blitt reveals the cloth that was covering Glenn Beck's bottom: a Klan hood (*left*). I talked to Zohar Lazar about showing terrorists in a cave watching Glenn Beck on TV (*opposite*): The idea was that they'd be rejoicing about the destruction they had wrought on America. But irony about the state of mind of a cartoon character is a hard concept to communicate visually: The reader can't help wondering, "What are all those people smiling at?"

WAR &
DISASTERS

ANA JUAN ON WAR & DISASTERS:

"As a working artist and illustrator, I don't usually get the chance to work on themes of war and disaster. It's a big challenge. Often the working time between when the disaster happens and when a sketch for a cover is due is very short—sometimes I only have a couple of hours to think.

"I think first of the message I want to convey. What do I want to say about the event? Once I figure that out, I begin to think about an image: Now I'm looking for an image that expresses my idea.

"When I try to find an image to represent a tragedy, I usually look at photos; it used to be from television or the newspapers, and now it's mostly from the Internet. I also look at cultural symbols, flags—anything that can represent a foreign country and can help inspire a cover. For this sketch (*opposite*), about the last conflict in Lebanon, I chose a palm tree as a symbol of the Mediterranean and drew bombs as its fruit.

"If you describe hard themes in a soft, serene voice, your message becomes louder. The beauty, by contrast, makes the horror more painful.

"Sometimes I'm grieving while I have to brainstorm, and since I am an emotional person, I discover things about myself I never imagined before. Some conflicts, tragedies, or disasters touch me more than others. I always want to do something with my work to help."

UNITED WE STAND

THERE WAS SERIOUS domestic opposition to the Bush administration's desire for war in Iraq, but it was quickly labeled anti-American. While some artists struggled to find images that would reflect their thinking without seeming unpatriotic, Barry Blitt, who still holds Canadian citizenship, didn't seem overly concerned about his patriotism being called into question: He drew all the opponents of the United States embracing one another while burning American flags, with of course a beret-wearing, cheese-eating sur-render monkey in the front row (right).

"WHEN THINGS ARE incredibly seri-ous you have to couch it in a different way," says Anita Kunz, who believes that "you can't really put blood and guts and gore on a magazine cover." In the sketch she handed in when George Bush ordered the invasion of Iraq, Kunz shows Bush literally putting his head in the sand (far left). Meanwhile, in response to the same event, Ana Juan finds a way to paint the blood and gore (opposite). Barry Blitt imagines Rumsfeld, Bush, Cheney, and Rice getting their kicks from watching the bombs drop away (left). Blitt says he was eager to do a color finish so he could highlight Condoleezza's dress with pink.

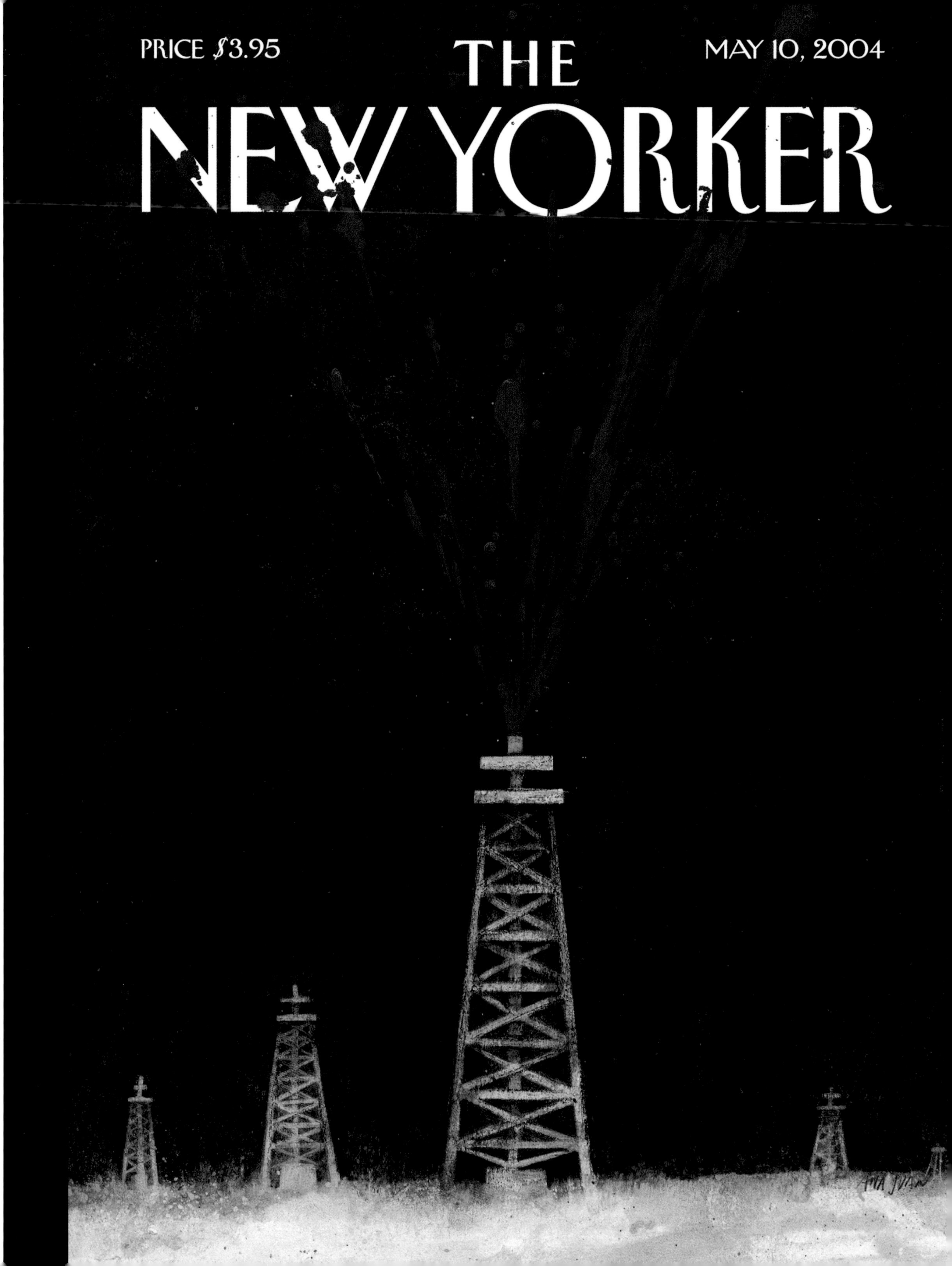

PRICE $3.95

THE
NEW YORKER

MAY 10, 2004

MUSLIMS AMONG US

"There isn't anything that's taboo for me. That would be making rules and I don't believe there are rules for humor. Once I think of an idea and it makes me laugh, I immediately think, 'Oh shit, they'll never go for this'—but I still send it in."
–BARRY BLITT

"I REMEMBER THE SUMMER leading up to 9/11, there was nothing to make jokes about—I was sort of bored," says Barry Blitt, who, like most of us, was left speechless by the early September events of that year. But by December of 2001, the media was in the throes of a campaign about "IT," a new device that would change our lives. *IT* turned out to be the Segway. It may not have had quite the impact predicted, but Blitt lost no time: He showed Osama bin Laden and his entourage escaping from the caves of Afghanistan on *IT* (*right*). Later, as the invasion of Iraq got under way, Blitt proposed the camel as the animal of choice for Central Park carriages (*below*).

IN 2002, semifinalists were named in the World Trade Center site design competition and models of the architecture firms' proposed projects were put on display, garnering comments by people from around the world. Ever disrespectful, Blitt sketched Osama bin Laden and his second-in-command reviewing the proposed designs (*opposite*).

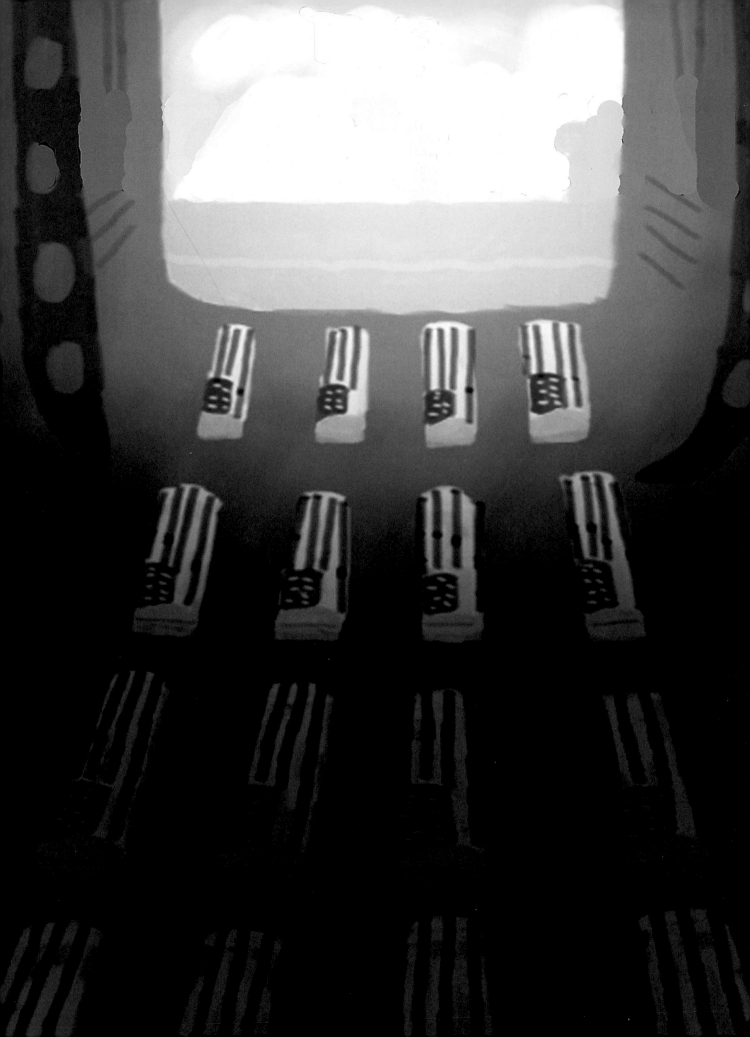

FREEDOM FRIES

THE STATUE OF LIBERTY variously appears as a symbol of America, of democracy, of New York—or is remembered as a gift from the French. Christoph Niemann and R. J. Matson submitted their sketches (*right and far right*) during the hysterical outbreak against the French led by the Murdoch press in 2003: The French were at that moment thought to be insufficiently enthusiastic about the U.S. invasion of Iraq. The restaurants that served the House of Representatives renamed French fries "freedom fries."

IN WARTIME, somber images, such as Lou Romano's flag-draped coffins shipped home by the military (*opposite*)—an image that had become rare since the Defense Department banned the media from photographing caskets during the first Gulf War—were interspersed with others where artists tried for laughs. A good topic for derision throughout was the motive underlying the new patriotism. Art Spiegelman, who strived to express his disaccord with virtually all of the policies of the Bush administration, used the iconic Uncle Sam from James Montgomery Flagg's World War I recruiting poster to paint what he saw as the United States' call to arms in the twenty-first century (*left*).

PREMATURE JET LANDING

IN 2003, PRESIDENT BUSH landed on the deck of the aircraft carrier USS *Abraham Lincoln* and gave a speech announcing the end of "major combat operations" in the War on Iraq, while standing in front of a "Mission Accomplished" banner. The staged event was a moment of compounded irony for those who remembered that young Bush had not distinguished himself during his own military service. Still, artists did their best to satirize the event: Owen Smith (*opposite*) had Bush giving the A-OK sign as he readied his plane to land on a panicked populace at the Washington Mall (the inspiration for this was a 1962 series of Topps "Mars Attacks" trading cards, *below, left*). Christoph Niemann had soldiers at Arlington Cemetery folding the "Mission Accomplished" banner in lieu of the American flag laid on a fallen comrade's coffin (*right*). Barry Blitt (*below, right*) had the battered president stagger in front of a banner for *Mission: Impossible*, the late-sixties TV series.

PRICE $4.95

THE
NEW YORKER

OCT. 18, 2004

ABU GHRAIB

THE HUMAN RIGHTS violations that took place at the Abu Ghraib prison in Iraq included homicide, torture, rape, and sodomy. The snapshot of a hooded prisoner who was made to stand, arms outstretched, on a cardboard box, attached to electric wires that would jolt him awake should he tire, became iconic. It kept appearing in sketches that I received at the time, and I painted it as a shadow on the American flag for the cover of the October 2004 special Politics Issue (*opposite*). Later, Philip Gourevitch, one of the *New Yorker*'s top reporters, who wrote a book on Abu Ghraib with documentary filmmaker Errol Morris, told me that the blanket thrown on the prisoner had been an act of kindness, provided by his torturer to keep him from getting cold. The use of hoods on prisoners appeared to be a return to medieval practices and the methods of the Spanish Inquisition. News photos, such as one on the front page of *The New York Times* of a soldier wiping his sweaty face with a flag (*far right*), also seemed to echo the same nightmare imagery. The hood haunted artists' sketches as well, such as these by Ana Juan (*below, right*), Mark Ulriksen (*below, top left*), and Anita Kunz (*below, bottom left*).

"What was happening had such profound implications, I really did want to make a commentary about it. Even in visual terms, in terms of design, just that triangle was so profound. I incorporated it with the scales of justice."

—ANITA KUNZ

LED ON A LEASH

THE ABUSE AND TORTURE of detainees committed by military personnel at the Abu Ghraib prison were detailed in the *Taguba Report*, an official Army military inquiry conducted in early 2004. But it took a CBS report and a story in *The New Yorker* by Pulitzer Prize–winning journalist Seymour M. Hersh to break the story to the country. For months, artists sketched, trying to understand and digest the unbearably shocking images that had been thrust into the public consciousness. It often felt more like an attempt at exorcism than at getting published. Barry Blitt didn't shy away from the totally outrageous when he drew Lynddie England (*right*) as a typical New York dog walker flashing a thumbs-up signal. Richard McGuire's painting (*opposite*) depicts the waterboarding of an upside-down prisoner. The scene, whose composition is inspired by Old Master paintings of the Deposition of Christ, is portrayed as emotionless and anonymous: Torturers wear hoods, and everyone's face, save for a medieval scribe's, is hidden.

MARCELLUS HALL'S reaction was typical of many other artists'. His first sketch of Bush holding the leash on Uncle Sam (*top*) spoke of the shame many felt when they saw the photos—though that image was too close to a political cartoon to work well as a cover. He later sent a sketch of Bush as Don Quixote (*above*), which was considered, so he did a finish (*right*). In that version, it's now Bush who is led on a leash by Cheney.

TOPPLING ICONS

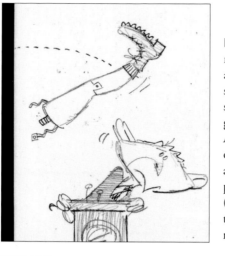

IN DECEMBER 2008, AN IRAQI journalist threw his shoes at President Bush during a press conference in Baghdad. The president swiftly ducked. As the incident gained widespread attention, Americans learned that the gesture is a traditional sign of contempt in the Arab world; Iraqis had thrown shoes at statues of Saddam Hussein after his overthrow. Quickly adopting the practice, Richard McGuire proposed a shower of shoes on the White House (*bottom, left*), and Bob Staake sketched a soldier throwing his artificial limb, complete with military boot, at the president's head (*left*).

IN A WIDELY TELEVISED event in 2003, a statue of Saddam Hussein in Baghdad was pulled off its pedestal by U.S. soldiers while a small crowd of Iraqis watched. Two years later, a local Baghdad cleric used the same square to stage a rally demanding the withdrawal of all the occupation forces. When Anthony Russo proposed an image (*opposite*) of Iraqis taking down an American soldier, in the spring of 2006, it was painfully close to the reality of the moment. By fall 2006, when Republicans lost their hold on Congress in the midterm elections, Mark Ulriksen used the same visual metaphor to show the toppling of a once mighty tyrant (*right*).

DIET COKE AND MENTOS

THE SPIRIT OF SCIENCE is alive and thriving, thanks to YouTube. In the fall of 2005, videos began making the rounds showing what happens when pieces of Mentos candy are dropped into bottles of Diet Coke: Each Mentos candy has thousands of tiny pits over its surface which become "nucleation sites"—perfect places for the carbon dioxide in the soda to form bubbles. The combination instantly triggers an explosion of foam (*right*). The phenomenon itself exploded, as YouTube users reenacted and improved on the experiment. There were videos in slow motion, two hundred liters of soda combined with five hundred Mentos mints, and a Guinness world record set by 2,865 simultaneous geysers.

© BRYAN BOWERS

IN DECEMBER OF 2009, a twenty-three-year-old Nigerian man on board a flight from Amsterdam to Detroit became known as "the underwear bomber" when he attempted to detonate explosives hidden inside his underwear, as parodied by Barry Blitt (*left*).

BARRY BLITT FIRST TRIED HIS IDEA with two children and then with two businessmen before finding the right and frightfully funny combination—two Arab men (*opposite*). All versions make fun of terrorism, but only that one makes fun of our own fears. In all instances, the co-conspirators look conspicuously guilty and make sure that the stewardess has safely passed. In the end, the image did not run out of a concern that the Diet Coke and Mentos reference may just have been too obscure for many of our readers.

TSUNAMI

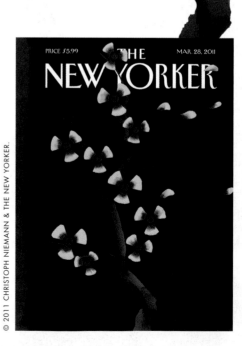

WHENEVER A MAJOR world event disrupts the news cycle, artists I work with know without asking that we'll be looking for ideas. The images here were sent to me very soon after an earthquake produced a tsunami that devastated Japan's northeastern coast on March 11, 2011. Ana Juan (*above, left*) used a limited palette and a red spot on the belt of a kimono. Japan seems to demand simplicity and spareness as well as the use of red, white, and black. Bob Staake colored Hokusai's *Great Wave* red (*above, right*), the same red that bathed Zohar Lazar's moonlit sea (*bottom, left*). Lorenzo Mattotti painted in stark black-and-white brushstrokes the desolate landscape left in the tsunami's wake (*opposite*).

JAPAN'S VISUAL CULTURE is rich in symbols, and many artists used similar imagery. In a sketch by Bob Staake (*above, left*), the Japanese flag's red circle becomes Sisyphus's boulder. *The Economist* ran a very similar image on their cover (*above*). While we were choosing among sketches, it became clear that the natural disaster had produced a man-made disaster of equal magnitude—a nuclear meltdown at the Fukushima nuclear power plant. Our choice as the cover for the following week, "Spring Blossoms" by Christoph Niemann (*right*), elegantly and eerily showed the confluence of the twin calamities.

© 2011 CHRISTOPH NIEMANN & THE NEW YORKER.

BIN LADEN

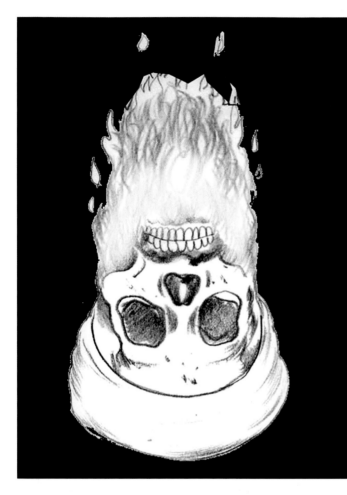

ON MAY 1, 2011, President Obama surprised the world with the announcement that Osama bin Laden had been killed by American forces. We learned that his shrouded body had been buried at sea. Harry Bliss's image (*opposite*) captured some of the somberness of death amid the jubilant celebrations that followed the announcement. It also doubled as a reference to the government's refusal to release photographs of Bin Laden's mutilated body. I was sent many images of Bin Laden in Hell, like Anita Kunz's image of a burning skull (*above*) and Barry Blitt's darkly funny sketch of Osama brushing elbows with Stalin and Hitler (*right*).

BOB STAAKE'S poignant image (*above*) of two planes flying between the Twin Towers showed a version of reality where the tragedy never happened. *Time* magazine's cover (*below, right*) referenced the cover they ran at the time of Hitler's death in 1945 (*below, left*). In the billboard-size version of it in Times Square (*left*), the windows double as bullet holes.

IS NOTHING TABOO?

ON COMING UP WITH IDEAS:

MARK ULRIKSEN: "Something will strike me as 'Oh! That could be a *New Yorker* cover!' and I'll jot the idea down on a scrap of paper. When I give myself a day or two to work on covers, I refer back to my notes. The news changes so quickly that some things have already passed. But there are other things that are timeless: political hypocrisy, the rich getting richer, prejudice. The cover of *The New Yorker* is like a captionless cartoon—you have to figure out: How do you boil something down to a single image?"

ART SPIEGELMAN: "I try to squelch my internal censors and just doodle, even if I don't agree with the politics of the doodler, until something comes into focus."

BARRY BLITT: "You have to use stereotypes to make a cartoon, you just have to. But how do you avoid tarnishing all people who wear little round caps on their head? I just don't worry about it—or I'll worry about it and then I think, 'Stop being an old lady,' to myself. 'Don't be so cautious here. Because otherwise you don't get any jokes.'
Still, every single cover I think, 'Oh, no! Now they'll come after me.' After the Ahmadinejad on the toilet, I was in my studio in the barn and I heard some craft overhead. I looked out the window and there was a helicopter with stars and stripes on it—it landed in my backyard. I thought the government was coming to protect me. But it was for medevac: There was a motorcycle accident down the road—it turns out our land is designated as a landing strip."

*The ballerina's "sudden jeté" by M. Scott Miller (opposite) predates the
Janet Jackson 2004 Super Bowl halftime wardrobe incident. It may simply
have been a facetious attempt on the part of Miller to show skin—though*

FOOD FOR THOUGHT

"Provocative images are necessary because we've all got our two-car garage and our fridge full of food, so there's complacency. We need to shake things up a little bit, and images have a unique way of doing that: We're a visual culture." —MARK ULRIKSEN

WHAT WE LAUGH AT evolves over time. As the number of obese and overweight people point to an epidemic that ravages the health and well-being of average Americans, a painting by Mark Ulriksen of overweight Americans in a high-wire act with fast food (*opposite*) and a sketch by Barry Blitt of Michael Moore sinking into the wet cement of Hollywood's Walk of Fame (*right*) cease to seem so funny. Lack of access to fresh produce and overconsumption of sugar and refined foods in the United States are deeply political issues, alluded to in Mark Ulriksen's painting of a starving child being handed some of the candy we lavish on our kids on Halloween (*below*). Anita Kunz's overweight Statue of Liberty (*middle, right*) is a problematic subject for a laugh when the drawing is all there is, though a similar image can be used if it's to illustrate a cover story (*bottom, right*).

"What are some things that remain taboo? People don't talk about money, people don't talk about class."

—MARK ULRIKSEN

EAST AND WEST

MANY ARTISTS STRUGGLE to make sense of the treatment of women in Islamic countries—Anthony Russo depicts a stoning (*left*), while Barry Blitt (*far left*) wonders how an artist can portray a woman hidden under a chador or burka. Zohar Lazar's image of gay U.S. soldiers in Afghanistan kissing (*opposite*) can be seen as either a celebration of tolerance in a repressive place or an example of America imposing its values where they are not welcome—or both.

THE MAGAZINE'S MASCOT, Eustace Tilley, usually examines a butterfly through a monocle. In John Mavroudis's twist (*above*), the covered "Eustacia" has no arm or hand to hold a monocle and her eyes are nearly closed. In another sketch by Zohar Lazar (*right*), Afghan soldiers are looking at photos of their wives . . . fully covered.

DEADLY ENCOUNTERS

CLICHÉS ABOUT DANGEROUS women abound. They inform Barry Blitt's image of a lipstick ammunition belt (*below*) worn by a former beauty queen thrust into the news as a born-again Christian politician from a remote state, who likes to brag about her familiarity with hunting weapons. Beginning in 2002, female suicide bombers had started to appear in the Middle East, taking advantage of the privacy rules, especially in the Islamic world, that make women less likely to be body-searched than men. Danny Shanahan situated his female bomber with a burka (an anachronism) on the subway grating of a busy New York street (*opposite*), which was of course the setting for Harry Bliss's aged Marilyn (*below, middle*) and for Barry Blitt's chador-wearing dame (*below, right*). Meanwhile, in a gratuitous sketch (*right*) by Blitt—who doesn't fly—Homeland Security's ever-stricter travel rules are enforced by a suicide belt–wearing officer checking an equally belted traveler while an airplane quietly blows up in the background.

TWO VIEWS of parents and children, one for Mother's Day, by Art Spiegelman (*above*), the other for Father's Day, by Barry Blitt (*opposite*), who says: "There are images I wish I hadn't done, but it's usually for aesthetic reasons. I don't really believe anything is genuinely offensive—who cares if somebody is offended: It's neither the goal nor a deterrent. I once sketched a cattle car going to Auschwitz: There was one guy talking on his cell and everyone was irritated—that was just to make you, Françoise, laugh, and you did. I'll make bad jokes—it's good to clear the air."

ACKOWLEDGMENTS

My biggest debt of gratitude goes to the artists, past and present, including those who are not in this book, but who all have taken up the challenge of making story-telling images. I'm especially grateful to Art Spiegelman, who introduced me to the universe of graphic art and encouraged me to explore in all directions; to Saul Steinberg who taught me how to edit images with Oxam's razor; and to Barry Blitt for making me laugh every time we talk. None of this would exist without the vision of *The New Yorker*'s editors Tina Brown and David Remnick. David Remnick not only provides incentives for the artists to take chances week after week, but he has always stood by what he publishes, often with remarkable courage. This book greatly benefited from his suggestions. I'm also grateful to Pamela Maffei McCarthy, *The New Yorker*'s deputy editor, for her support and her eagerness to see the covers get their due. I owe a large debt to Andrew Wylie, my champion, for his trust and support and for getting the project into the hands of Eric Himmel, editor extraordinaire at Abrams. Eric's guidance and unwavering trust navigated this project through many storms and delivered it to safe harbor. My grateful thanks to Tamara Arellano and Kara Strubel at Abrams, who polished the draft; Eric Rayman, who contributed his guidance, knowledge of funny people, and legal expertise; Jonathan Bennett, who advised about design; Peter Canby, who recommended Julie Tate and to Julie Tate for her expert fact-checking; Greg Captain, for his expertise on the production of the covers; and to Kate Welsh, Emily Kan, Mina Kaneko, Emily Viemeister, and Leigh Stein for their help with the logistics and for their correspondence with the artists. And last, but not least, I'm immensely grateful to my *bras droit*, Nadja Spiegelman, who provided everything this project needed at every turn: discussions that allowed the chapters to find their shape, interviews with the artists, corrections of the drafts, and trust in the outcome. Nadja's intelligence, sense of humor, and superb writing skills substantially improved this book. If it's any good, it's thanks to the artists, thanks to Eric Himmel and to David Remnick, and very much thanks to Nadja.

SHORT BIOGRAPHIES

ISTVAN BANYAI was born in Budapest, Hungary, in 1949, moved to Paris, Los Angeles, and Manhattan, and now lives in rural Connecticut. His illustrations appear in *The Atlantic, Rolling Stone, The New York Times*, and many others. Banyai has illustrated record cover art and has animated short films for Nickelodeon and MTV Europe. His 1997 children's book, *Zoom,* was chosen as one of the *New York Times* 10 Best Children's Books. He has done ten *New Yorker* covers since 1998. For him, doing covers for *The New Yorker* is a "masochist trip and challenge . . . I call it No Yorker."

BARRY BLITT was born in Montreal, schooled in Toronto, and burnished to a gleaming shine in New York. His work has appeared in a wide variety of publications such as *Vanity Fair, The New York Times, Entertainment Weekly*, and many others. He's the author or illustrator of many children's books. Blitt has done sixty-eight covers for *The New Yorker,* the first being "Resolute Smokers," published in 1994. For Barry, "Doing covers for *The New Yorker* is/was/would be delicious/less filling."

JOHN CUNEO was born in Westfield, New Jersey, in 1957 and currently lives in Woodstock, New York. His drawings have appeared in many publications, including *The Atlantic, Esquire, Vanity Fair*, and others. He is the recipient of gold and silver medals from the New York and the San Francisco Society of Illustrators. Cuneo has done two covers for *The New Yorker*, the first one being "Flu Season" in 2009. For Cuneo, doing covers for *The New Yorker* "means you get seven full days to think about why the damn sketch was better than the final."

HARRY BLISS was born in Rochester, New York, in 1964 and now lives in Burlington, Vermont. He is a recipient of many awards for his cartoons and his children's books. His single-panel gag cartoon, "Bliss," appears daily in over fifty newspapers. Bliss has done twenty covers for *The New Yorker*, the first being "The New Year" in 1998. For him, working for *The New Yorker* is "Insane! Its high rejection rate has toughened my artistic skin." Still, from day one, Bliss says, "*The New Yorker* has inspired the best of my creative output and it always will . . . until the day the rejection finally kills me."

R. CRUMB was born in Philadelphia in 1943 and currently lives in the south of France. He is best known for his creation of *Zap Comix* and *Weirdo*, as well as his comic book characters Fritz the Cat and Mr. Natural. In 2009, he published a comic book rendition of the Book of Genesis. He's done two covers for *The New Yorker*, the first in 1994. He is currently serializing excerpts from his diary in *Mineshaft* magazine. For Crumb, working for *The New Yorker* "evokes a complicated mix of conflicting emotions."

PETER DE SÈVE was born in Queens, New York, in 1958 and currently lives in Brooklyn. His work is featured in magazines, books, print and television advertising, as well as animated films, such as *Mulan, A Bug's Life*, and *Finding Nemo*. He designed the characters for the three blockbuster *Ice Age* movies. He also recently collaborated on his first children's book, *The Duchess of Whimsy*, with his wife, Randall. De Sève has done thirty-two covers for *The New Yorker*, the first in 1993. For him, doing covers for *The New Yorker* "would be great if it happened more often."

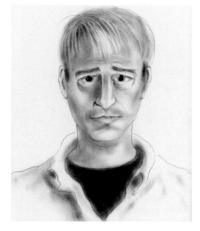

IAN FALCONER was born in Connecticut in 1959 and now lives in Greenwich Village, in Manhattan. His children's books starring Olivia, which he began as a present to his niece, earned him the Caldecott Medal and a Gold Award from Parents' Choice. He has designed sets and costumes for operas and theaters including the Royal Opera Covent Garden and Paris's Théâtre du Châtelet. Since 1996, he has done twenty-nine *New Yorker* covers. For him, doing covers for *The New Yorker* "*can* be a joy . . . depending on the taste and sense of humor (or lack thereof) of the current editor."

CARTER GOODRICH lives and works in Los Angeles. Since 1995, he has been an art director and character designer for many animated features, including *The Prince of Egypt*; *Finding Nemo*; *Monsters, Inc.*; and *Despicable Me*. After four nominations, his designs for *Ratatouille* won him the Annie Award in 2007. Since 1994, Goodrich has done sixteen *New Yorker* covers. For him, doing covers for *The New Yorker* is "a way to still claim the city as home, even from three thousand miles away."

ANA JUAN was born in Valencia, Spain, in 1961 and currently lives in Madrid. Her work has appeared throughout the U.S., Europe, and Asia and is regularly published in *El País*. Juan's illustrated books and children's books include *The Night Eater*, which won the Ezra Jack Keats Award. In 2011, Juan won the National Illustration Award given by the Spanish Ministry of Culture. Juan has done nineteen *New Yorker* covers since 1995. For Juan, doing covers for *The New Yorker* is "a challenge."

GREG FOLEY was born in 1969 and currently resides in New York City. His designs have been exhibited at MoMA and at Paris's Pompidou Center. He's the author of the award-winning children's books *The Willoughby and the Lion* and the *Thank You Bear* series. He was a Grammy nominee for Best Recording Package for *Release* by the Pet Shop Boys. He's the creative director of *Visionaire*, *V Magazine*, and *VMAN*. Foley started submitting work to *The New Yorker* in 2011. For him, doing covers for *The New Yorker* would be "even better than doing covers of Abba songs."

MARCELLUS HALL was born in Minneapolis and now lives in New York City. His work regularly appears in publications such as *The Wall Street Journal*, *The Atlantic*, and *The New York Times*. He has illustrated children's books for Abrams and Simon & Schuster. As a musician, he has recorded with the bands Railroad Jerk and White Hassle, and released a solo album, *The First Line*, on Glacial Pace Recordings in 2011. Hall has done two *New Yorker* covers. For him, *The New Yorker* is "the only job where the prestige rivals the payment."

ANITA KUNZ was born in 1956 in Toronto, where she currently resides. Her work is regularly published in *TIME*, *Rolling Stone*, *Vanity Fair*, and many other publications. Kunz was the first Canadian, and the first woman, to have a solo show at the Library of Congress's Swann Gallery. She was appointed an Officer of the Order of Canada and won a lifetime achievement award from the Advertising and Design Club of Canada. She's done eleven covers for *The New Yorker*, the first one in 1995. For Kunz, doing covers for *The New Yorker* is "a great way to contribute to a wider conversation about politics and culture."

ZOHAR LAZAR was born in Israel in 1971 and moved to New York in the '80s. He uses a range of media, from traditional oil painting to ink wash, and also makes comics. His work is exhibited in galleries and appears in many publications, as well as on his blog and on the Meathaus website. He contributed artwork for a number of releases by the band They Might Be Giants, including "The Spine," "Prevenge," "Experimental Film," and "Au Contraire" singles. Lazar did one *New Yorker* cover, in 2009. For him, it was "much better than doing a *New Yorker* cover exercise in art school."

R. J. MATSON was born in 1963 in Chicago and raised in Brussels, Belgium, and Minneapolis. He currently resides in St. Louis. His work is published in the *St. Louis Post-Dispatch* six days a week and in *Roll Call* four days a week. One of his works was named *TIME*'s best editorial cartoon of the year in 2007. Matson did one *New Yorker* cover, in 2000, titled "Six More Weeks of Primaries." For him, doing covers for *The New Yorker* is "a childhood dream fulfilled."

JOHN MAVROUDIS was born in 1962 in California, where he still lives. He's the art director of the California Film Institute. As an artist and designer, he created over two dozen posters for the legendary Fillmore poster series. He cocreated (with Owen Smith) one *New Yorker* cover, in 2006, showing tightrope artist Philippe Petit high above the footprint of the World Trade Center. It was named cover of the year by ASME and one of the ten best covers of the year by *Advertising Age*. For him, "having *The New Yorker* as your canvas means reaching the pinnacle of illustration."

JACQUES DE LOUSTAL, born in 1956, is a cartoonist and illustrator who lives in Paris. His extensive traveling through Africa, South America, and Asia is reflected in his many books of travel sketches. He began doing comics in the late 1970s, publishing in magazines such as *Metal Hurlant*, *Rock and Folk*, and *À Suivre* in France, and *RAW* in the U.S. He has done eight covers for *The New Yorker*, the first one in 1993. For Loustal, doing covers for *The New Yorker* is "the grail for an illustrator—any illustration is better with the *New Yorker* logo on top."

LORENZO MATTOTTI was born in Italy in 1954, and currently lives in Paris. He is a comics artist and illustrator who contributes to *Vogue*, *Le Monde*, and *Vanity* (Italy). He has written and illustrated many graphic novels, including *Dr. Jekyll and Mr. Hyde*, for which he received the Eisner Award in 2003. Since 1993, he has done twenty-six covers for *The New Yorker*. For him, doing covers for *The New Yorker* is "a game of chance, but it's worth it."

RICHARD McGUIRE is a renowned musician, designer, animator, and cartoonist, as well as an author of both children's books and experimental comics. His work appears in a wide variety of publications, including *The New York Times*, *McSweeney's*, *Le Monde*, and *Libération*. He has designed and directed animated films. He's the founder and bass player of the punk-funk band Liquid Liquid. He recently cowrote and directed the closing piece of the French animated feature film *Fear(s) of the Dark*. Since 1993, McGuire has done sixteen covers for *The New Yorker*. For him, doing covers for *The New Yorker* is "a warm puppy."

M. SCOTT MILLER, born in 1969, began his art career in New York after graduating from the Pratt Institute. He's now back in his hometown of Missoula, Montana. His work has appeared in a variety of publications, including *The Village Voice*, *The New York Observer*, *Popular Mechanics*, and several children's books. In 2012, he will have a one-man show at the Missoula Art Museum. Miller has done three covers for *The New Yorker*, the first in 1996. For Miller, doing covers for *The New Yorker* was "my big break."

ERIC PALMA was born and raised in New York, where he currently lives. His caricatures and humorous line drawings have appeared in a broad range of publications, including *Entertainment Weekly* and *Smithsonian*. Palma has received awards from the Society of Publication Designers, *Art Direction* magazine, and the Society for News Design. He did one cover for *The New Yorker*, in 2004. "It was thrilling. Throughout that week, I got so many calls from friends and family wondering if I was the same guy who drew the cover."

LOU ROMANO, born in 1972, is an art director who lives in San Rafael, California. He has been published in *Written By*, the magazine of the Writers Guild of America. In addition, he has copublished two books, *The Ancient Book of Myth & War* and *The Ancient Book of Sex & Science*, with Pixar Animation Studios colleagues. In 2005, he received the Annie Award for Production Design on Pixar's *The Incredibles*. He did one cover for *The New Yorker*, in 2007. For him, doing covers for *The New Yorker* is "a wish come true."

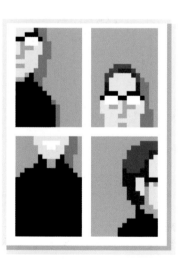

CHRISTOPH NIEMANN was born in 1970 in Germany, where he currently lives with his wife and three sons. He is an illustrator, graphic designer, author, and coauthor of several books, including children's books. In 2010, Niemann was inducted into the Art Directors Club Hall of Fame. He's been the author of the *New York Times* blog *Abstract Sunday* since 2008. He has done sixteen covers for the *New Yorker*, the first in 2001. For him, doing covers for *The New Yorker* is "very, very difficult."

ROBERT RISKO was born in Pennsylvania in 1956, moved to New York City at age nineteen, was discovered by Andy Warhol in 1978, and hasn't stopped working since. He regularly publishes in magazines such as Andy Warhol's *Interview*, *Vanity Fair*, *Rolling Stone*, *Playboy*, and *Esquire*. He is the author of *The Risko Book* and *Vanity Fair's Proust Questionnaire*. In addition, Risko has created movie and theatrical posters as well as icons for VH1 and the Kennedy Center Awards. He has done four covers for *The New Yorker*, the first in 1992. For him, doing covers for *The New Yorker* is "THRILLING!"

ANTHONY RUSSO was born in 1949 and currently spends most of his time in Rhode Island. He is a regular contributor to *The New York Times*, *The Los Angeles Times*, *The New Republic*, and *The Boston Globe*, among many others. He has received numerous awards from Communication Arts, American Illustration, Society of Illustrators, Graphis Annual, Society of Publication Designers, Art Directors Club, and several other organizations. Russo did one *New Yorker* cover, in 2003. For him, doing covers for *The New Yorker* is "very challenging."

DANNY SHANAHAN, a cartoonist, currently lives in Rhinebeck, New York. His illustrations have appeared in *The New York Times*, *The Wall Street Journal*, *TIME*, *Newsweek*, *Playboy*, and *Esquire*, among many others. His cartoons are in the permanent collection of the James Thurber Museum, and have appeared in dozens of collections, including four of his own. Shanahan has done ten covers for *The New Yorker*, the first in 1990. For him, doing covers for *The New Yorker* is "challenging, fun, and a great way to make complete strangers mad at you."

OWEN SMITH was born in California, where he still lives. His work has appeared in numerous publications such as *Rolling Stone*, *Playboy*, *GQ*, and *Esquire*, as well as on book jackets and in children's books. He designed mosaics for Brooklyn's Thirty-Sixth Street subway station. He illustrated Aimee Mann's album *The Forgotten Arm*, which won a Grammy for best packaging. Since 1993, he has done seventeen *New Yorker* covers. "It was always a dream of mine. When Françoise first called, I put on my most calm and professional voice. But when I hung up, I began screaming and jumping up and down like an idiot. If she'd seen me then, she would have had her doubts."

ART SPIEGELMAN, the Pulitzer Prize–winning author of *Maus*, was named one of *Time*'s 100 Most Influential People in 2005 and received the Angoulême International Comics Festival's Grand Prix in 2011. He has done thirty-nine *New Yorker* covers. For him, doing covers for *The New Yorker* is "a source of great pride—it's amazing to see one's work under the same logo as Addams, Arno, and Steinberg!—and an ongoing frustration, since it involves submitting work to editors (including my spouse!) . . . and I just don't submit to others easily."

BOB STAAKE was born in 1957 in Los Angeles, and currently resides in Cape Cod. He is a frequent contributor to *The Washington Post*, *The Wall Street Journal*, and the *Los Angeles Times*, among other publications. He has written and illustrated many children's books, including *The Red Lemon*, which was chosen as a *New York Times* Best Illustrated Children's Book. Since 2006, he has done twelve *New Yorker* covers. For him, it is "like playing Carnegie Hall: I'm always relieved if I didn't play a false note—or spill ink."

MARK ULRIKSEN is a former art director turned illustrator. Born in 1957 in San Francisco, he has been living there, in the Haight-Ashbury neighborhood, for the past twenty-five years. His drawings appear in numerous publications such as *The New York Times* and *The Washington Post*. He has received gold and silver medals from the Society of Illustrators. Since 1994, he has done thirty-eight covers for *The New Yorker*. For him, doing covers for *The New Yorker* is "the best, coolest, and most lasting thing that has happened in my career."

self portrait 1978

BOB ZOELL (HA) is a fine artist and designer who has had a forty-five-year art career in Los Angeles and now lives in Pasadena, California. His work has been shown in Japan, France, and throughout the United States. He's the recipient of the Pollack-Krasner Foundation and the Adolph and Esther Gottlieb Foundation grants. His work *"BFILRYD" (Bird + FLY)* was installed at the San Francisco International Airport in 2010. He's currently involved with many public art projects. He has done seven covers for *The New Yorker*, the first in 1994. For him, doing covers for *The New Yorker* is "a lot of fun."

INDEX

Abu Ghraib, 101, 102
Addams, Charles, 86
Ahmadinejad, Mahmoud, 12, *14*, 15, 113
Arab Spring, 88
L'Assiette au Beurre, 6, *6*
Avedon, Richard, 8

Banyai, Istvan, 30, 31, *31*
  biography, 123
Beck, Glenn, 88, *88*, 89
bin Laden, Osama, 94, *94*, 95, 110, *110*
Bliss, Harry, 24, *25*, 36, *37*, 86, *86*, *87*, 110, *111*, 118, *118*
  biography, 123
Blitt, Barry, 4, *4*, 5, *5*, 6, 12, 14, *14*, 15, 16, 20, *20*, 24, *24*, 27, *27*, 34, *34*, 36, *36*, 38, *38*, 39, *39*, 42, *42*, 43, 49, 50, *50*, 51, 53, *53*, 54, 55, *55*, 56, *56*, 57, 57–59, 64, *64*, 65, 66, 68, 69, 70, *70*, 72, 73, 74, *74*, 77, *77*, 80, *80*, 81, 82, 83, 84, *84*, 85, 86, *86*, 88, *88*, 92, *92*, 94, *94*, 95, 99, *99*, 102, *102*, 106, *106*, *107*, 110, *110*, 113, 115, *115*, 116, *116*, 118, *118*, 120, *121*
  biography, 123
Boyle, Susan, 86, *86*
"Bradley effect," 55
Breitbart, Andrew, 36
Briggs, Korwin, 88, *88*
Britain's Got Talent, 86
Brokeback Mountain, 50, *50*
Brown, Tina, 7, 8, 20, 66, *66*
Bush, George W., 24, *24*, 52, 53, *53*, 60, *60*, 64, 66, *66*, 92, *92*, 98, 99, *99*, 102, *102*, 104, *104*

Carlson, Gretchen, 57
Catholic Church child-abuse, 42
Chauncey, George, 12
Chavis, Benjamin, 23
Cheney, Dick, 50, *50*, *51*, 64, *64*, 92, *92*, 102, *102*
Chessum, Jake, 60, *61*
Chomsky, Noam, 10
Clinton, Bill, 32, *32*, 34
Clinton, Hillary, 34, *34*, 55, *55*
Clowes, Dan, 6
Colbert, Stephen, 60, *61*
Coppertone, 88, *88*
Cotton, William, 8, *8*, 44, *44*
Coulter, Ann, 57, *57*
Craig, Larry, 12
Crumb, R., 39, *39*
  biography, 123
Cuneo, John, 62, *63*, 82, *82*
  biography, 123

The Daily News, 59
Deposition of Christ, 102
Diallo, Amadou, 8–9
Diet Coke, 106, *106*, *107*
Donohue, Bill, 44
Don Quixote, 102, *102*
"Don't Ask, Don't Tell," 39
Drudge Report, 58

The Economist, 108, *108*
Edward VII, 6, *6*
Eisenstaedt, Alfred, 39
England, Lynndie, 102, *102*
Entertainment Weekly, 60, *61*
Esquire, 32, *32*

Falconer, Ian, 17, *17*, 39, *40*, 41
  biography, 124
Fey, Tina, 64
Flagg, James Montgomery, 97
Flynt, Larry, 34
Foley, Greg, 20, *20*
  biography, 124
Fox & Friends, 57
freedom fries, 97
Freedom from Want (Rockwell), 46, *46*
Friedman, Drew, 70, *70*

Gaines, James R., 23
Galliano, John, 20
Gates, Henry Louis, Jr., 24, *24*
Gibson, Charles, 64
Giuliani, Rudy, 8–9, 24, *25*
Glover, Danny, 24
Goldman, Ronald, 23
Goodrich, Carter, 12, *12*, 26, *26*
  biography, 124
Gourevitch, Philip, 101
Ground Zero mosque, 27

Hall, Marcellus, 102, *102*
  biography, 124
Hersey, John, 7, *7*
Hersh, Seymour M., 102
Hitler, Adolph, 74, *74*, 110, *110*
Huffington Post, 57
Hussein, Saddam, 104, *104*
Hustler, 34

Iraq invasion, 92, *92*

Jackson, Janet, 113
Jackson, Michael, 78, 79, 80, *80*, 81
Juan, Ana, 70, *70*, 90, 91, 92, *93*, 101, *101*, 108, *108*
  biography, 124

Kennedy, Ted, 36, *36*
King, Larry, *54*, 55, *55*
King, Martin Luther, Jr., 84, *85*
Kruger, Barbara, 30, *30*
Ku Klux Klan, 23
Kunz, Anita, 10, *10*, 32, 73, *73*, 92, *92*, 101, *101*, 110, *110*, 115, *115*
  biography, 124

Lazar, Zohar, 88, *89*, 108, *108*, 116, *116*, *117*
  biography, 125
Leibovitz, Annie, 66, *66*, 82, *82*
Lewinsky, Monica, 32, *32*, 34
Limbaugh, Rush, 44, 49, 57, *57*, 59
Lincoln, Abraham, 70, *70*
Louima, Abner, 24
Loustal, Jacques de, 10, 12, 13, *13*
  biography, 125

MAD, 73, *73*
Mahurin, Matt, 23

Matson, R. J., 58, *58*, 97, *97*
  biography, 125
Mattotti, Lorenzo, 15, *15*, 108, *109*
  biography, 125
Maus, 7
Mavroudis, John, 60, *60*, 84, *84*, 116, *116*
  biography, 125
Mazzucchelli, David, 10, 11, *11*
McCain, John, *54*, 55, *55*, 60, *60*, 62, *62*, 66, *66*, 67
McGuire, Richard, 102, *103*, 104, *104*
  biography, 125
Mentos, 106, *106*, *107*
Middleton, Kate, 84, *84*
Miller, Scott, 12, *12*, *112*, 113
  biography, 126
Moore, Michael, 115, *115*
Morris, Errol, 101
Mouly, Françoise, 16, *16*, 57–59, *100*, 101
  biography, *122*
My Pet Goat, 64

The Nation, 53, *53*
National Enquirer, 58, 82
Neuman, Alfred E., 53, *53*
Newsweek, 23, *23*, 63, *63*
New York Post, 9, 10
New York Times, 58, 101, *101*
Niemann, Christoph, 52, 53, 97, *97*, 99, *99*, 108, *108*
  biography, 126

Obama, Barack, 24, *24*, 49, 50, 55, *55*, 56, 57, *57*, 58, 59, 66, 69, 70, *70*, 71, *72*, 73, *73*, 74, *74*, 77, 110
Obama, Michelle, 56, 57, *57*
O'Reilly, Bill, 57, *57*

Palin, Bristol, 66
Palin, Sarah, 62, *62*, 63, 64, *64*, 65, 66
Palma, Eric, 64, *64*
  biography, 126
Panter, Gary, 7, *7*, 15, *15*
Powell, Colin, 24, *24*

RAW, 7
RAW 1: The Graphix Magazine of Postponed Suicides, 6, 6
RAW 3: The Graphix Magazine That Lost Its Faith in Nihilism, 7, 7
Remnick, David, 5–6, 8, 29, 32, 42, 58, 84
Rice, Condoleezza, 24, *24*, 92, *92*
Richards, Michael, 84, *85*
Risko, Robert, 70, *70*, *71*, 78, 79
  biography, 126
Rockwell, Norman, 44, *44*, 46, *46*
Romano, Lou, 76, 77, *96*, 97
  biography, 126
Roosevelt, Franklin, 70, *70*, 71
Rove, Karl, 53
Rumsfeld, Donald, 92, *92*
Russo, Anthony, 104, *105*, 116, *116*
  biography, 126

Safir, Howard, 10
Salon, 32

Santa, 44, *44*, 80, *80*
Saturday Evening Post, 44, *44*, 46, *46*
Saturday Night Live, 64
Saying Grace (Rockwell), 46, *46*
Schwarzenegger, Arnold, 84, *84*
Segway, 94, *94*
Seinfeld, 84
Sève, Peter de, 30, *30*, 63, *63*
  biography, 123
Shanahan, Danny, 118, *119*
  biography, 127
Shawn, William, 7
Sheen, Charlie, 88, *88*
Simpson, Nicole, 23
Simpson, O. J., 23, *23*
Smith, Owen, 28, 29, 98, 99
  biography, 127
Sorel, Edward, 8
Spiegelman, Art, 6, *6*, 7, 8–9, *9*, 16, *16*, 18, *18*, 19, 20, 21, *21*, 23, *23*, 24, *24*, 32, 33, *33*, 34, *35*, 36, *36*, 42, *42*, 44, *44*, 46, *46*, *47*, 62, *62*, 97, *97*, 113, 120, *120*
  biography, 127
Spitzer, Eliot, 30
Staake, Bob, 69, *69*, 73, *73*, 74, *75*, 104, *104*, 108, *108*, 110, *110*
  biography, 127
Stalin, Josef, 110, *110*
Starr, Kenneth, 34
Statue of Liberty, 97, *97*, 115, *115*
Stauffer, Brian, 69, *69*
Steinberg, Saul, 9, 64
Stewart, Jon, 60, *61*
Stop Islamization of America, 27
Strauss-Kahn, Dominique, 34, *34*

Taguba Report, 102
Tea Party, 74, *74*, 75
Tilley, Eustace, 19, 116, *116*
Time, 23, *23*, 42, *42*, 70, *70*, 74, *74*, 110, *110*
Topps Mars Attacks trading cards, 99, *99*
Trump, Donald, 84, *84*

Ulriksen, Mark, 30, *30*, 39, *39*, 50, *50*, 53, *53*, 55, *55*, 101, *101*, 104, *104*, 113, *114*, 115
  biography, 127
Uncle Sam, 97, *97*, 102, *102*
underwear bomber, 106, *106*
USS *Abraham Lincoln*, 99

Vanity Fair, 66, *66*, 82, *82*
Visionaire, 20

W, 30, *30*
Walmart, 44
"War on Christmas," 44
Weiner, Anthony, 36, *36*
William (Prince), 84, *84*
Woods, Tiger, 82, *82*, 83
World Trade Center
  1993 bombing, 10
  2001 attacks, 15, 64, 94
  site design competition, 94, 95

Zoell, Bob, 22, *22*, 23, 30, *30*, 44, *45*
  biography, 127